JUST GO!
A Global Guide to
Budget Travel

JUST GO!
A GLOBAL GUIDE TO BUDGET TRAVEL

Enhanced and Enlarged Edition. 2015

JOHN P. CROSS

JUST GO! A GLOBAL GUIDE TO BUDGET TRAVEL
ENHANCED AND ENLARGED EDITION. 2015

iUniverse books may be ordered through booksellers or by contacting:

iUniverse
1663 Liberty Drive
Bloomington, IN 47403
www.iuniverse.com
1-800-Authors (1-800-288-4677)

ISBN: 978-1-4759-7195-8 (sc)
ISBN: 978-1-4759-7196-5 (e)

Library of Congress Control Number: 2013900959

Printed in the United States of America.

iUniverse rev. date: 01/28/2015

JOHN P. CROSS

John Cross currently lives in Atlanta, Georgia, which serves as his base camp for travel. Atlanta has an exceptional airport with worldwide connections. The author has traveled completely around the world to all seven continents, including Antarctica and the Arctic. Altogether, Cross has been to more than seventy countries, and he has traveled the Trans-Siberian Railway from China and Mongolia to Moscow and St. Petersburg in Russia.

Cross has an M.A. in history and two minors in geography and Spanish. He is a former teacher and a publishing sales representative. Travel is his passion.

> "If you reject the food, ignore the customs,
> fear the religion, and avoid the people, you
> might better stay at home."
> —James Michener

To my mom, dad, and sister

CONTENTS

PREFACE

"Travel is fatal to prejudice, bigotry, and
narrow mindedness, and many of our people
need it sorely on these accounts. Broad,
wholesome, charitable views
of man and things cannot be acquired by
vegetating in one little corner of the
earth all one's lifetime."
—Mark Twain

Just Go! will be of interest to the armchair traveler or
the traveler who is contemplating a trip. It includes
trip-planning budget ideas and travel tips that will inspire
and motivate the would-be traveler.

While the book does not include every country in the
world, it does integrate history and culture throughout the
narrative, lending a global view and allowing the reader to
develop a respect for the culture of other peoples. It is not
ethnocentric.

Just Go! has many competitors; Lonely Planet and
Frommer's travel guides are the foremost. I firmly believe
the intrepid traveler will find this book inspirational and
motivational.

This travel book is the culmination of my life experiences
of "man meets world." May you benefit from what I have

learned. There is no limit to the beautiful travel memories you may accumulate in your lifetime of travel.

I simply recommend that if you get an idea for travel, you should just go! You will have a world of experiences and memories. Follow your dreams. Happy travels!

> "He who is outside his door already has the
> hardest part of his journey behind him."
> —Dutch Proverb

1

Budget Travel: A Guide to the Essentials

"Travel is like an endless university.
You never stop learning."
—Harvey Lloyd

Just Go! is a compilation of what I have experienced and learned over the years during my travels. Most of my trips were abroad, although I have traveled most of the US. The premise of my book is that anyone who is motivated to travel, regardless of his or her place in life, is capable of traveling to any destination he or she chooses. One does not need to be a wealthy person to pursue his or her travel dreams. Whether one is a backpacker, a teacher, or a manager, with proper planning and budgeting, he or she can travel far.

The most expensive part of a trip is usually the airfare. This is where the personal computer comes in handy to find the best prices. One of my favorite online booking websites is KAYAK; I use it for both domestic and international flights. KAYAK searches all the airlines and compares the airfares. Recently, KAYAK introduced an upgrade—the new site is named KAYAK.com/explore, and it displays a world travel map on your computer. It is also interactive. You simply move the arrow on the travel map to your desired destination and the airfares appear. You still have the option of using KAYAK.com. Other similar websites are SideStep.com and Vayama.com. I have also used Travelocity, Hotwire, and Priceline. Expedia is another one. Charter group flights such as Apple Vacations can be a frugal alternative.

Another discount company with travel deals is Friendly Planet Travel. 1-800-555-5765. They offer discounted tours to Thailand, China, Turkey, and Greece. They also offer trips to a number of places worldwide. Check out their catalog on Google for a viable travel option during hard economic times.

A website which is fast becoming a favorite of mine is ITA Software.com by Google. It is especially good for searching for international airfares. It is referred to as a matrix airfare search. Like KAYAK, it gives you comparative airfares. However, you cannot book your ticket with ITA. After finding the best airfare, go to an agent or website to book your ticket. I find ITA extremely helpful.

A travel agent usually charges you a modest fee but can save you time and effort. On some occasions I use a travel agent because he or she can often find a ticket from a "discounter" for overseas travel. These tickets are usually nonrefundable. Be sure to buy travel insurance, found through companies such as World Nomads or Travel Guard Chartis. Make sure the travel agency is a member of ASTA, a professional society.

One of my favorite travel websites is lonelyplanet. com/thorntree. This website is extremely useful for anyone planning or researching a trip location. The format is mostly question and answer. For example, if you are planning a trip to Mexico, you simply log into the Mexico site and ask your question. Fellow travelers will offer you answers and solutions for your trip. This website covers the entire world. I like the category called "Traveling on a Shoestring" for questions about the economics or financing of travel. Try it. I think you will find it very useful.

I came across an article in *Condé Nast Traveler* regarding airfare tips that I wish to pass along. The article is called "The Top Five Secrets to Savvy Travel: Save Big Now on Time and Money."

The article suggests that you fly on a Tuesday, Wednesday, or Saturday to save money. These days are off-peak times and mean lower fares. Next, buy airline tickets midday on Tuesdays. That is when the most sale tickets hit the system after Monday nights. *Condé Nast Traveler* suggest you book flights and rooms for Saturday, Sunday, and Monday for the best deals and that you use your credit cards that earn you travel rewards. You will receive special rates and perks. Finally, *Condé Nast Traveler* suggests you use the most experienced travel representative when booking a trip. This person can get you the most perks such as upgrades.

Students and teachers often have some advantages when booking budget-class airfares and hotels. For instance, consider STA Travel for discount booking; you'll need STA identification and discount cards. STA is a member of ABTA, IATA, and ASTA. You can visit your local STA Travel store or call 1-800-781-4040. STA has negotiated travel discounts on many of the world's top airlines. It also provides discounts for motels and hostels in the US and worldwide. Sign up for their newsletter.

Another card I recommend for students is the International Student Identity Card. This card provides excellent discounts on hostels, transportation, and entertainment. Go to isic.org for more information. Sometimes you can buy the card at your first hostel stay.

Teachers may consider international teacher-led educational tours with EF. Teachers travel free when they enroll at least six students. EF has been partnering with educators for forty-five years. Contact EF at 1-877-316-2051 or eftours.com. They offer a free brochure.

The cost of your hotel will be your next biggest expense. Again the internet is a traveler's best tool for finding the best budget hotel or hostel. Google is always your best bet, but you can use Bing as well—just type in the name of the city. TripAdvisor is another good search site. You can also try Mobissimo, which is similar to KAYAK. Mobissimo helps you find cheap airline tickets, airfare, and discount hotels. It is very thorough and compares hundreds of airlines and hotels.

Your next expenses will be eating and drinking. My best suggestion is to try to eat and drink with the locals when possible. You need to find smaller restaurants with lower prices and fixed menus. Many times I have purchased my food at a grocery store and consumed it in the room with wine or picnicking in a park. Try to use a quick language guide when possible or just observe what the locals are eating. In Europe, the breakfast is often included in the room rate. Also, consider making lunch your big meal of the day. The price of a carafe of wine is cheaper than a corked bottle. Beer is usually inexpensive, so you might consider taking a winery tour or brewery tour.

In general, you can keep prices down by traveling during the off-season and veering away from the beaten path. Always try to haggle or negotiate the price of the room. Perhaps there is an off-season discount? If you are a student or senior, always ask for a discount. And always get a receipt.

Touring will be your next expense. If you are not in a tour group, I suggest using public transportation when possible to keep costs down. Most cities, especially in Europe, offer day passes or weekly travel passes for public transportation such as the train, the metro (or subway), and the public bus line.

Walking tours are an excellent way of touring a city. Tourist information booths will often provide a free tourist booklet or city maps for walking tours. Some of my best and most memorable experiences have happened while lost during my walking tour. Walking tours also provide opportunities to mingle with the people.

Flea markets are a great way to go shopping on a budget; plus shopping there is a cultural experience. The best bargains are found here rather than at department stores. Remember to bargain for the best prices. Start by setting your goal at 50 percent of the vendor's asking price. Then bargain your way up until the vendor agrees on the price. This is especially important in Mexico.

Getting cash is easier when using ATMs, but beware of the bank fees. Traveler's checks are the safest way to travel with money. However, not everyone will take traveler's checks nowadays. Credit cards are increasingly being accepted overseas. They can also be used for cash advances. Always remember you will be charged a usage fee for cash advances. Let your bank know you will be traveling.

Transportation in Europe for intercity travel is easy and affordable. The options in Europe are rail, bus, or discount airlines. The rail network is extensive in Europe and is probably the best and most affordable transportation for intercity travel. Eurail is the name of the European rail service. You can book your train ticket in the US before you leave by using the STA travel office. Another way to book your European train ticket is through the Rail Europe site. The train is a great way to enjoy the scenery.

Budget airlines can save you time and money on intercity travel, especially in Europe. With deregulation, the no-frills airlines are appealing. The best examples in Europe are Ryan Air, Air Berlin, and Easy Air. Ryan Air is based in Dublin. Air Berlin makes its hub in the Berlin-Tegel airport.

Taxis, trams, metros, and buses are available in the cities when you arrive.

The taxi is another means of transportation within the cities. It is more expensive but faster when you need to travel in a hurry. Many people assume a taxi will most likely rip off the rider by taking the long route or not using the meter. It is best to ask the taxi driver to use the meter or at least agree upon a price before taking the taxi ride. The driver can be a good source of information.

Travel by bus is a viable alternative for budget travelers. The bus offers low-cost fares and gives you a freedom and flexibility not offered by other modes of transportation. Bus travel is especially popular in Europe.

Eurolines buses or coaches are most popular in Europe. This bus line offers a Eurolines Pass, which provides unlimited travel among fifty-one cities across Europe and gives the traveler the flexibility to plan his or her route while traveling. The Eurolines Pass is available for a fifteen- or thirty-day duration. The fifteen-day pass costs 180 Euros. Point-to-point tickets are also available. Travel by bus lacks the charm of the train, but the bus is a useful, scenic way to cross Europe.

Make sure you have an updated passport before traveling abroad. You should make a backup copy of the passport before departure. Some countries may require an entrance visa, which you can purchase by mail before leaving home.

Many countries, such as in Chile, allow you to purchase the entrance visa at the airport when you enter the country.

You are now ready to travel! Pack light; always be aware of your surroundings; try to mingle with the people and enjoy the culture of the country.

Happy travels!

2

Computer Apps: The New World of the Mobile Device in Travel

"Getting information off the internet is like
taking a drink from a fire hydrant."
—Mitchell Kapor

Apps have become popular in the travel world today. No discussion of travel is complete without the use of Apps in travel planning and touring. There are Apps for almost every aspect of travel. Apps are used mostly on smart phones, Iphones, Android, Ipod, and tablet. In other words, mobile devices. There are Apps for ticketing, hotel rooms, and mapping on GPS, news, and translation. Just about whatever subject you can imagine. New ones come out every day. I will only attempt to cover the most important ones for travel today.

What is an App? App is computerese shorthand for a software application program. Typically it is a small,

specialized program downloaded onto a mobile device such as a GPS app for your iPhone. It is important to be web savvy these days.

How do I install Apps on my smart phone or mobile device? There are various app stores. Use google to explore your options. Many people use the iTunes app store. You simply open iTunes to buy and download apps.

Log into your iTunes account which you create. Then click on the iTunes store and click the link at the top that says App Store. Then select the apps that you want and download and install the program. You will have to sync the mobile device and the app will appear. iTunes is probably the easiest way to add apps to your mobile device. Many are free to download.

Apps can also be found at Google and Apple. Some people have more than 100 apps on their iPhone. Lonely Planet offers downloads at lonelyplanet.com/mobile. Now let's look at some examples.

Kayak has an app for the Smart phone and tablet which can be downloaded from the Apple store for Apps. Kayak allows you to search for the best airline fare by comparing different airline's prices in seconds. You can find your flight, the hotel, and even manage your itinerary, or track your flight status. Kayak is a free app available for the iPhone, iPad, Android, Windows phone7, and Kindle devices. It is probably the number one mobile travel app.

Tripit app allows you to find your reservation and organize your itinerary. You can even get directions to your hotel. Tripit has all the information you need to get you where you're going and back again at your fingertips. Tripit can be used on the Smartphone or Tablet. Easy to use

Tingo is an app developed to help the traveler find a hotel. You simply book a hotel by destination. Select a "price drop" room and if the rate drops after you book, Tingo will refund the difference. Tingo is part of the "Travel Advisory" group.

Yelp is a great way to find restaurants, bars, cafes, and almost any business. Just push the "nearby" button and Yelp will search for you.

Translation Apps. Google Translate is a popular language translation app. An internet or WiFi connection is needed. More than sixty languages can be translated with Google Translate. In most languages it has voice capabilities. Simply speak into your Smartphone and it will turn your words into the language of your choosing. An invaluable mobile device!

CNN App for iPhone. CNN App can be downloaded using iTunes on your computer. CNN is a free app. CNN connects you to the world no matter where you are. It is an easy way to stay informed with the latest headlines from around the world. You can also download BBC News with iTunes. The New York Times has an iPad news app.

Pocket Earth. When using Pocket Earth you will never get lost again. This app contains almost unlimited interactive maps. You can access maps and travel guides. It is available on Apple for $2.99 USD.

The Weather Channel App is one of the best for determining the weather at your destination. It is a free download on iPad and iPhone. This app delivers weather forecasts, videos, and the most up-to-date weather maps. This is like having a weather station in your pocket. Indispensable for a trip!

Another weather app is Weather + Free. This app is in English no matter your destination. It gives you the local time, temperature, humidity, and other key factors regarding your destination.

How to get a cab? You can use your smartphone to get a cab. Options available are Uber and Taxi Magic.

When traveling overseas, it is always difficult to convert currencies in your head when shopping for that souvenir object you desperately want. Oanda Currency Converter App solves this problem. It can be used on your smartphone. Conversions can be made quickly and accurately. You will no longer overpay for your purchase.

International SOS has a travel assistance app for travel insurance covering worldwide emergency and evacuation services. Also, they can assist in lost passports. It is a one-click dialing to the nearest SOS Assistance Center for when the member traveler needs medical or security help. SOS can help business and organizations protect their employees around the globe. SOS can give you quotes at https://buymembership.internationalsos.com/ or call 1-800-523-8662.

One of my favorites is Trip Advisor. This app gives you travel reviews. It will help you find flights and hunt for a hotel.

Seat Guru is for use with the iPhone or Android. This allows you to find the best seats on the plane, search for flights, and low fares. For example, you can select the seat with the most legroom for your category. You can also search for flight status updates. It is a free download and a division of Trip Advisor.

As you can see, there are almost unlimited App Travel Sites. They will aid you in finding the best travel deals. A well-stocked mobile device is as essential as a passport. There are almost too many choices available.

Summary of Travel Apps

1. The Google Translate app allows a person to speak into the phone and get the information translated.
2. Oanda for converting currency. It is a free app available for the iPhone, Blackberry and Android. Rates updated daily.
3. International SOS is for travel insurance and covering worldwide medical and security help.
4. Hotels Tonight App for Google and Apple locates a room as much as 75% off for that night.
5. Umbrella Worldwide Weather App free on iTunes. Just click on the weather map for your location.
6. Trip Advisor's App. This can give you a list of things to do in your chosen city. Next to Google Earth this is the world's second most popular travel app.
7. Yelp is good for finding a business such as bars or cafes.
8. Google maps provides you with maps and distances for your city or destination.
9. Tripit organizes your flight and travel information.
10. Lonely Planet and Fodor's offers apps and eBooks for travel. Just pick your city.
11. Google Earth. This allows the traveler to see the world at street level. It literally flies you around the planet to the location you wish to explore. It gives you virtual tours in 3D imagery.

3

Mount Kilimanjaro, Tanzania, Africa: One Step at a Time

"A journey of a thousand miles must begin
with a single step."
—Lao Tzu

At 19,341 feet, Kilimanjaro is the highest mountain in Africa. The Europeans gave the Swahili name to the mountain in 1860. When the first missionaries saw the mountain, they were amazed that a mountain located almost on the equator could be covered by snow and ice. Hans Meyer, a German, was the first European to climb Kilimanjaro. He successfully climbed Kili, the mountain's nickname, in 1889. Uhuru Peak is the highest summit. Ernest Hemingway wrote about the mountain in *The Snows of Kilimanjaro.*

I traveled to Tanzania, once a German colony before the English took over after World War I, for a safari and to climb Kilimanjaro. The climb is not technical; it's more of a trek.

First I visited Arusha, and then I went on to Marangu. The Marangu route is the most popular tourist trek. It is a relatively easy route for the ascent and descent. The Frankfort Zoological Society has built a series of wooden huts along the route to accommodate the trekkers. You will need to hire a guide or join a travel group for your trek.

The trek starts out easily, passing through the tropical zone. But you should plan to be in good physical shape to climb the mountain. You will meet people of all ages along the way, and you will share the sleeping huts with others as you climb. Your guide will prepare your meals.

Most people think that, because it is a trek, there is no risk. But there is a prevalent risk of altitude sickness. This usually means shortness of breath, hypothermia, and headaches. If you experience this in your climb, you will need oxygen or to descend immediately. Deaths do occur. Your doctor can prescribe Diamox to help you adapt.

To prepare for the final ascent, one needs to become acclimated to the altitude. Mountain climbers use the term "climb high and sleep low." This is a good practice as you ascend. There are also pills you can take to help you adapt. Try not to ascend too quickly. Do not drink alcohol on the way up. The Marangu route usually lasts about six days-four days up and two days back.

The climber ascends through several temperature zones. At about 12,000 feet, climbers will be above the clouds with fantastic views. This is the ideal point in the trek to practice "climb high, sleep low." From here, climbers can continue to the base camp at the Kibo huts.

At the base camp, climbers bunk in a dormitory atmosphere. All groups are together. Climbers are served dinner and then turn in to prepare for the trek to the summit the next day.

During my climb, I did not sleep much in anticipation of the challenge facing me the next day. They woke me up at midnight to begin my final trek. Out we went. If all went well, we would arrive at the top at about six am to see the sunrise over the plains of Africa. The goal seemed near and excitement prevailed. The trek would take about six hours and was almost straight up. But still, it was trekking and not technical—one foot in front of the other, over the loose growth and volcanic rocks.

About halfway up, we came to a cave. I stopped there to catch my breath. There were two English couples in the cave having tea and cookies. They invited me to join them. It was very nice. I relaxed and got my courage up again. I thanked them and continued upward. I later saw them at the end of my trip and thanked them for reviving my efforts.

I continued to climb, one step at a time. At six am, I reached Gilman's Point, just short of Uhuru Peak. Once at Gilman's, I asked a French couple to take my photo, and then I continued on to the snowcap and glacier near Uhuru Peak, the very top. *All my training and effort has paid off,* I thought as the sun rose over Africa. *What a view! The plains of Africa under the morning sun!* I reached to drink some water, but the water was frozen in my bottle.

After enjoying the view from the top, I started my descent back to base camp and beyond. I had a spark in my walk, one of pride in my achievement. Climbing Kilimanjaro was an unforgettable experience. It ranks up there with getting my graduate degree. There were times I thought about quitting. *No one will ever know—but I'll know.* So I kept on, one step at a time.

Persevere and you will get there. It is easy to quit. Keep going and you will reach your goal; this is an important lesson in life.

4

Cabo San Lucas, Baja California Sur, Mexico: Gringo Paradise

"I haven't been everywhere,
but it's on my list."
—Susan Sontag

Cabo San Lucas began as a Spanish Colonial village founded by Hernán Cortés after he received a report that a shipwrecked sailor told of a land south of California that was rich in gold and pearls. Cortés sent ships in 1535 to explore the new land. They found no gold, but they did find pearls. The town of La Paz was established on the Sea of Cortez, or Gulf of California, east of the peninsula. Baja was now officially on the map.

In 1539, the Spanish explorer Francisco de Ulloa sailed south around the cape, and Cabo San Lucas was founded. Cabo San Lucas became a popular stopping point for Spanish ships as they sailed eastward from the Philippines. In Cabo San Lucas, they could resupply with water and supplies to continue their journey. They could also trade silk and spices from their trade routes in the Far East.

In the 1950s, Cabo became a place to see and be seen by Hollywood stars such as John Wayne, Bing Crosby, and Desi Arnaz. They rented a small plane and flew south along the Pacific coastline. The roads in Cabo were not developed. When the pilot saw no more land, it was time to land. Even today, Hollywood stars flock to Cabo. They go to the Cabo Wabo night club and the beach. Today, Cabo has numerous golf courses, and sport fishing there will always be an attraction.

The cape is called Finis Terra, or the end of the land. The distinctive arch, or El Arco, can be seen at the end of the Cabo San Lucas peninsula. El Arco is a popular tourist attraction. It can be reached by boat. Today, giant cruise ships stop in Cabo San Lucas.

The Mar de Cortez is a good hotel choice for budget travelers. A standard single room with a patio overlooking the pool is fifty-one US dollars. The location is in El Centro Cabo San Lucas on Lazaro Cardenas and Vicente Guerrero. Tel: 624143-0232. It is an easy walk to the marina and numerous restaurants and bars. This hotel was built in 1958. It is a piece of history.

The Mar de Cortez has its own restaurant and bar, Baja Peppers. It is popular with locals and gringos because of its large all American breakfast for thirty-five pesos, or three dollars. The best deal in Cabo, this breakfast comes with three eggs, bacon, country fried potatoes, fruit, and toast. The Baja Peppers is open for lunch and dinner. Also there is a daily happy hour with drink specials. Wine lovers will enjoy the wine cellar and extensive wine list. They feature weekly dinner specials such as ribs, pasta, soup, and salad. Monday is ladies night, featuring 50 percent off the menu.

Across the street from the Mar de Cortez is the famous Cabo Wabo bar and night club. This is the place for those who want to party like a rock star all night long. Cabo Wabo is owned by Sammy Hagar, a rock star from the United States. It features live music and is located on Calle Lazaro Cardenas and Guerrero. Tel. 624 143 1198. It is open nightly from seven pm to two am and includes a restaurant. There is a happy hour from nine am to four pm.

One of my favorite places to go in Cabo is the Giggling Marlin Bar and Grille. They call it the home of the Skip and Go Naked. It is located on Boulevard Marina and Matamoros, not far from the marina. Tel. 624 143-06-06. Website: gigglingmarlin.com. It features a nightly floorshow, good margaritas, typical bar food, sports on the television, and Mexican food. The staff is friendly.

A must stop for anyone going to Cabo, day or night, is El Squid Roe Cabo, which has a great dance floor. It is party city and features rock and pop music. It is open daily from eight pm to four am. Dinner is served until eleven thirty pm. It is located on Boulevard Marina, Plaza Bonita, Cabo San Lucas.

Baja Cantina in the Marina is one of my favorite places for happy hour and watching the ships in the marina. It is a dockside bar with sports on the TV that appeal to gringos. Baja Cantina features an all-day happy hour. The restaurant offers seafood and discounted bar snacks.

Another favorite of mine for dining is the Crazy Lobster Bar and Grill. Open day and night, it is located on Hidalgo Street across from Pancho Villas. Tel. 143-6535. Steaks, chicken, tacos, hamburgers, and BBQ ribs are offered at reasonable prices for family dining. It always seems to be crowded. If you catch fish and bring it to them, they will prepare it.

For beach fun, go to Medano Beach. Mango Beach Bar and Grill and the Office are the best places for margaritas, food, and people watching. Mango has a two-for-one happy hour from seven am to seven pm every day. From Medano Beach you have a great view of the rocky shore across and south of the marina. And you can see the Arch, or El Arco.

I recommend a day excursion, approximately a one-hour trip, to Todos Santos, north of Cabo on the Pacific. Todos Santos is a small colonial town of artists and latter-day hippies. The streets are lined with small boutiques, a church, and a Spanish plaza. Todos Santos is the home of the famous Hotel California, and to visit it is to go back in time. Some call Todos Santos "*el pueblo mágico*," the magical village. There are fourteen square blocks in the historic center of Todos Santos—art galleries abound. There are many restored historic buildings.

Todos Santos is the home of the annual Festival de Cine Todos Santos, a film festival. Also, there is a small history and culture museum. For lunch in Todos Santos, I suggest the Tequila Sunrise Bar and Grill in the center of town on Calle Juary near the Hotel California.

In the winter months, I suggest going whale watching in Cabo San Lucas. That's when the whales migrate around Cabo and travel up into the Sea of Cortez to mate. There are many options for whale watching tours. I recommend either Cabo Expeditions or Cabo Escape. They depart from the marina.

Cabo Escape offers sunset and snorkeling cruises. They can be contacted by your hotel or at 624 105 0177. You can find them at caboescapetours.com.

Cabo Expeditions is also known for its whale watching tours. They can be contacted at 624 1432700 or caboexpeditions.com.mx.

A trip to Cabo is an unforgettable travel experience. Los Cabos, the main town in Cabo San Lucas, is called the crown jewel of the Baja Peninsula. The popular Medano Beach is beautiful. There is world class sport fishing, whale watching, snorkeling, and golf. Cabo is also known for its wild and crazy nightlife where one can party like a rock star. There are many choices for activities. Cabo San Lucas is no longer just a sleepy fishing village. When you return home you will have a lifetime of memories. Enjoy!

5

Sicily. Palermo to Catania
Archaeology and Culture

"Two roads diverged in a wood and I—
I took the one less traveled by, and that has
made all the difference.
—Robert Frost

My travel to Sicily was a small group travel tour arranged by Gate 1 Travel in the U.S.A. There were only six in the group and the transportation across the island was in a new Mercedes SUV-Type van. The guide was a Sicilian named Giacomo. He was very knowledgeable and courteous. There is an advantage to having a local guide. You know where to visit and do not waste time. We were also given some days at leisure which allowed me to explore, shop, and sidewalk café sit to watch the passing parade of people. Also to enjoy the wine, coffee, and pastries.

The tour started with a tour of Palermo in Northwest Sicily. My air flight was on a combination of Delta, KLM, and Alitalia. My hotel in Palermo was the Mecure Palermo Centro, via Mariano Stabile 112, Palermo 90139, Italy.

The Hotel Mercure is in a great location and is within walking distance of most city attractions. The hotel is clean and well maintained. There is WiFi in the reception and a breakfast was included in the rate. The rooms were spacious. The average rate for a single was $178.00 USD and $202.00 for two in a double room. My room was prepaid at the group rate. The Mercure is a good choice when visiting Palermo. Via Mariano Stabile 112, 9013 Palermo. Tel +39 091/324911. Booking @ mercurepa.com. The Mercure is a 4-star hotel with 93 rooms. It is near Massimo. Ideal for business and tourist stays.

Sicily is the largest island in the Mediterranean. It is twenty minutes by ferry to mainland Italy and is the largest region of Italy. Messina is the closest city in Italy. Sicily has its own elected president but is an autonomous region of Italy. Sicilians are citizens of Italy. The total population is about five million people. The capital is Palermo.

Sicily has a rich and complex history because it was settled and occupied by many groups of ethnic people. Phoenicians 734 B.C. After the Phoenicians, first to colonize Sicily were the Greeks in 750 B.C. Romans came next followed by the Vandals. The Arabs and Normans arrived next. Arab Sicily lasted from 827-1091. Norman Sicily was 1061-1194. In 1860, Giuseppe Garibaldi captured Sicily and it became part of Italy. Italian unification followed a vote to unify with Italy. Technically it was part of the Kingdom of Sardinia.

As a result of its history, Sicily reflects in its culture and architecture a diversity not found elsewhere. It is a compilation of the Greeks, Romans, Byzatines, Spaniards, French, and Normans. Each contributed to the culture of Sicily.

In touring Palermo, one can see the results of a history of foreign domination and mixed culture. The blending of cultures can be seen at the Catredrale, or Cathedral. In Italian, it is the Duomo. The architectural style is a blend of Byzantine, Arabic, and Norman. The original site was a Muslim Mosque which was built over a Christian Basilica. In 1184 the Normans modified the site by building their version of a Cathedral. Bell towers were added. Eventually a dome was built. Truly this represents eclectic architecture which is a result of a series of rebuilding, additions, and modifications over many centuries.

The interior of the original building was different from the present one. In the 18th century it was divided into nave and aisles by a series of pillars. A series of chapels were created. Located at Corso Vittorio Emanuele, Palermo. Tel 091-334373. Just follow via Vittorio Emanuele from North to South. It will be on your left after Via Maqueda.

An easy and economical way to tour the major tourist locations is by taking the Hop On—Hop Off Palermo sightseeing bus. You can't miss the bright red bus. There is line A and line B. The cost is about 20.00 Euro. It is an open-top, double-deck bus. You can board at any stop such as Teatro Massimo, Palazzo Reale, or Cathedrale. Tel. +39 09 1589429, or info Palermo @ city-sightseeing.it.

Next stop was the Duomo di Monreale. This cathedral is a must visit. Monreale is a short drive out of Palermo. It is considered the most important Norman Cathedral. Built in the 12th century, it is a beautiful blend of Byzantine, Norman, and Arab influences.

On entering, you immediately see 42 huge golden Byzatine Mosaics depicting Old Testament scenes. The altar area is also impressive. Also, notice the Arabic tiles on the floor. It is stunning and well worth the drive. The Monreale

Duomo is considered a national monument of Italy and one of the most important attractions of Sicily.

A little known fact is that the heart of Saint Louis is preserved in the Monreale Duomo. The address is Piazza Gulielmo 11, 1 Monteale, Province Palermo. Tel +39 091 6402424.

An exceptional architectural site to visit in Palermo is the Teatro Massimo Opera House which opened in 1897. It is the largest opera house in Italy. The perfect acoustics is renowned throughout Europe. The opera house was dedicated to King Victor Emanuel II. The address is Piazza Giuseppe Verdi, 90138 Palermo. Tel +39 091 6053580. Check the time for tours of the opera house. Rigoletto was presented while I was in Palermo.

Sicilians like to dine. For pizza, there are many choices. I recommend Frida Pizzeria located at Piazza Sant Onofrio 37, 90100 Palermo. Tel +39 091550 5440. It is in the neighborhood of Sera l cadio just off via maqueda. The food is excellent. The ingredients are fresh and there is a large selection of combinations. Service was fast and efficient. Just ask for Antonio. Prices at Frida Pizzeria were moderate. Prices range from 9 USD to 20 USD. Beer and wine are available.

One of the outstanding Palermo restaurants is Cin-Cin. This is a favorite with locals. Outstanding Sicilian food. It is located at Via Manin 22, Palermo. Tel+39 091 612 4095. It is family operated by Vincenzo Clemente. Cin-Cin is considered a moderate priced restaurant. Prices ranging from 12 USD to 22 USD.

Cin-Cin serves up great seafood. The swordfish filet is especially good. Pastas are popular. They are known for their homemade gelatos. Other popular foods are Panelle, or fried chick pea pancakes, and crocchette, or croquette potatoes. The ambiance and great food make Cin-Cin a must stop in Palermo.

No trip to Palermo is complete without sampling the pastries and ice cream. For this I suggest the Bar Café Alba. Located at Piazza Don Bosco near Via Liberta and Viale Lazio. I discovered Alba by accident when I was walking down Via Liberta. I stopped in for refreshments. Alba is an institution and is usually crowded with standing room only. They have great pastries, ice creams, and finger foods. Coffee is served as well. It is typical Sicilian pastries. As they say in Sicilian, "Divino!"

Shopping is a favorite pastime of the Sicilians. Tourists also enjoy shopping and bringing home memories from Sicily. Some tourists seek out the famous name brands from Italy such as the leather goods of Gucci or Luis Vuitton. You can find most whatever you desire by walking down Via Liberta. But be prepared to pay since these are glamorous flagship brand shops.

My special interest was the Gucci flagship shop because my lady friend had placed a special order with me before leaving on my trip. Gucci is located at Via Della Liberta 37, 90139 Palermo. Tel. +39 091.585687. The shop covers two floors. The prices are too expensive for me ranging from 895 to 1295.00 Euros. But the visit to Gucci is an experience in itself.

I did not buy my lady friend a Gucci bag in Palermo. I waited until we were traveling toward Catania. Before you reach Catania, just off the highway is the popular Sicilia Outlet Village. The village contains a variety of shops selling at a discounted price, products of such retailers as Gucci, Versace, Armani, Calvin Klein, and Trussardi. Some items are discounted as much as seventy percent.

By the way, I discovered there is a free shuttle service upon reservation, reaching a minimum of thirty passengers every day of the week from Palermo, Catania, Agrigento, Siracusa, and several other cities. Tel. 39 0935 950040. info@siciliaoutletvillage.it. www.siciliaoutletvillage.it.

The outlet village has over 100 shops. You can finally afford to buy yourself the high fashion items you have always wanted. There are also cafes and restaurants. "The only difficult thing will be going home empty handed."

Gucci handbags today have become a fashion prestige item. They can be worn for years without going out of date. Guccio Gucci, the founder, opened his first leather shop in 1921 in Florence, Italy. Gucci designed high-end leather goods such as luggage and expanded into handbags. Today the Gucci symbol is internationally respected and famous.

How do you tell if a Gucci bag is authentic? The buyer wants to make sure they get what they are paying for since it is an expensive investment. First, look inside the bag at the interior label. All Gucci bags are made in Italy. Make sure the bag has a cont-rollato card inside. This is the inspection sticker for a Gucci bag. Lastly, examine the Gucci logo. It should be two letter Gs, almost touching, with one upside down. You do not want to overpay for a fake bag like you would buy in Chinatown, NYC.

Back in Palermo, the Ballaro market is a popular place to visit for shopping, dinner, or just sightseeing. It is located at Palazzo Reale. Ballaro is probably the best market to visit in Palermo. It is quite crowded and noisy. There are numerous fish and vegetable stalls. Many locals do their shopping here. It is a great market for browsing.

From Palermo, my travel group travels southwest to the coastal town of Marsala, about seventy seven miles by auto. Marsala is a port city with fertile soil to produce the world famous Marsala wine. The city is a popular stopover for a visit to the Valley of the Temples.

The Hotel Dio Scuri Bay Palace was our base in Marsala. It is located at Lungomare Falcone, Borsellino 1, 92100, San Leone, Sicily. Tel. +39 0922 406111. info@ dioscurihotel.it. A great location for visiting the Valley of Temples. The rooms are moderately priced. About 86 Euros per night.

Out next visit was to a winery in Marsala, the Florio Winery founded in 1835. They produce fine Marsala dry wine. Marsala wine, originally a sweet wine, is made only in Western Sicily. It is considered Italy's finest wine. After a tour we were served lunch with wine in a delightful historic building.

Marsala wine was first introduced to the world by an Englishman, John Woodhouse. His ship had to take shelter in the port. That night while visiting a Marsala tavern, he first tasted Marsala wine. He was so impressed he took some bottles home with him and the world got to know Marsala wine. Be sure to visit one of the many wineries.

Wine is most popular in Sicily but they also have their favorite beers. Peroni beer was founded in 1846 in Italy and is based in Rome. After growing in popularity in Italy, it expanded into foreign markets. Today it is the most recognized and most widely consumed Italian beer. The lager brand has a heavy finish but not too strong.

Surprisingly Ceres beer, imported from Denmark, has a large following in Italy and Sicily. It is a strong ale but does not taste too heavy because raw grain has been used to soften the taste. It is medium body and goes well with Mediterranean food, cheese, meat, and pizza.

Next we travel along the Southern Coast to visit the Valley of the Temples in Agrigento. This is on the road to

Catania. It is almost the same route General Patton took when liberating Sicily from the Nazis in WWII. Although he was traveling in the opposite direction from Catania to Palermo.

The Valley of the Temples is one of the most impressive sites I have seen in my travels around the world. It was an inspirational site and has been named a UNESCO world heritage site in 1997. A bit of trivia is that the Temples are not actually located in a valley but rather along a ridge outside Agrigento.

Altogether, there are eight temples in the historical site in the valley. All of the temples are in the Doric architectural style. The temples were built in the 5th century B.C. by the Greeks. The Romans arrived later and restored the Temples to their original Doric style.

The two primary temples are the Temple of Concordia and the Temple of Castor and Pollux. The other temples are Temple of Juno, Temple of Heracles, Temple of Zeus Olympia, Temple of Vulcan, and Temple of Asclepius.

To visit the Valley of Temples and the museum you need to buy a combination entrance ticket. The price is 10 Euros. There is an entrance gate.

The Temple of Concordia is the best preserved of the Doric Temples. It dates from 430 B.C. during the Greek period. Later in the 6th century, it became a Christian Cathedral which is why it was saved from destruction.

The Temple of Castor and Pollux is another favorite of the tourist, a must photograph. It is all that remains from a temple built in the 5th century B.C. It has been restored by an architect. The temple is composed of four Doric columns. It is the most photographed and has become the symbol of the town of Agrigento. You will see this temple on every post card from Agrigento.

Be sure to take time to visit the Archaeological Museum at the end of your tour of the Valley of Temples. Many consider it the best museum in Sicily. A visit here puts the Temples into proper historical perspective. A must visit for the serious tourist.

Back on the road again. My tour group heads for Catania. Our last stop on our tour of Sicily. We make a short detour off the Palermo-Catania highway (A19) to visit the Sicilia Outlet Village. This is where I eventually found my affordable Gucci bag.

Our hotel in Catania was the excellent Una Hotel Palace. It is a member of the prestigious Una chain. It is centrally located on the major street, Via Etnea, 218-95131 Catania, Italy. Tel. +39 095 2505111. Una.palace@unahotels.it. www.unahotels.it. My room was the largest room I have ever occupied in a hotel. It was magnificent! Single 150 Euro. There are two restaurants, outdoor pool, health club and spa. The roof garden bar has an excellent happy hour with free food to sample. The UNA is considered to be a four-star hotel.

The most prominent historical landmark is the Catania Cathedral or Duomo. This structure also includes The Chapel of Sant' Agata. It is an easy walk from the UNA Hotel. Catania is an easy walking city. From the hotel, take the main street, Via Etnea. Walk toward the Porto and arrive at the intersection of Via Victoria Emanuele II. There stands the Duomo at the Piazzo Duomo.

The Duomo of Catania was built in the 12th century. It had to be entirely rebuilt after the Mt. Etna volcano eruption and earthquake which destroyed most of the city in 1669. Inside the cathedral you will find the Chapel of Sant' Agata. It is named for the city's patron saint. The architecture of the Duomo is most impressive. It is Sicilian Baroque.

In the front of the cathedral is the Piazza Duomo, or cathedral pedestrian square. The Plaza is a popular gathering spot for locals. In the center of the Piazzo Duomo stands a statue called Catania's Elephant. It is the symbol of Catania. On top of the elephant is an Egyptian Obelisk. This represents the influence from Asia and Africa upon the history and culture of the city.

The elephant is made of volcanic stone dating from the Roman period. Legend has it that the monument contains some magic or mystic powers. Some say the statue represents good luck against any future eruptions of Mt. Etna.

At the far side of the Piazza is the famous fountain, Fontana dell'Amenano, fed by the Amenano underground river. This also marks the entrance to the Fish Market. The market during the day is always crowded and noisy. A stroll through the market is a sensation for the sight and smells.

There are several sidewalk cafes in the Piazza Duomo. Great for taking a break to have cake and pastries, or a coffee, or wine. There are several souvenir shops. Great for watching the passing parade of people. A shop for souvenirs is Sicilia in Tradizione. Plaza Duomo, 14 (dietro Fontava dell' Elefante) Tel 095 25 03007 Catavia.

Along Via Etnea, a worthwhile place to visit is the Benedictine Monastery. This is a religious building but looks like a palace. Today it is associated with the University of Catania and serves as faculty offices.

The Teatro Massimo Bellini is an interesting visit in order to see its splendid auditorium. Historically it is important because it is named for Bellini, the great opera composer from Catania. Bellini was original buried near

Paris but his remains were transferred to his home in Catania.

A visit to Mt. Etna makes a good day trip. Going up the mountain, you can see the lava flow from past centuries. Usually there is a snow cap at the top. The elevation is 10,920 feet and is the highest and most active volcano in Europe. There is a cable car at the top. Shops and restaurants are also available to visit. It is popular with skiers and hikers.

A travel company in Catavia called Escursion Sull' Etna offers tours for 49 Euros. Another travel company is Sikania Excursions. Their price is 50 Euros. Sikania can be reached at Tel. 39 349 5465488. Excursion in Sicily is Tel. 39 095 8362956. Of course, your hotel can make the reservation for you. Groups travel cheaper.

Food and dining are important in the lives of Sicilians. This is true with Catavian citizens. There are ample restaurants and cafes to choose from.

People who like pizza should try Eat Pizzeria, via Pietro Antonio Coppola, 42 95131 Catavia. Tel 39 095 310100. The food and service is excellent. Be sure to meet Giuseppi, the owner. The Pizza Margherita gets good reviews. The menu has 45 pizzas. They also serve pasta. The menu is reasonably priced. It is popular with both locals and tourists.

If you prefer a trattoria, then I recommend the Trattoria Catania Ruffiana, Via Aloi, 50, Catania. Tel 0952 162222. The pasta is popular. Marco is the maitre de. The menu is Mediterranean and the squid and mussels are popular. Dessert is free.

For pastries, I recommend the Gelateria Quaranta, Piazza Mancini Battaglia, Catarina. It is noted for its ice cream and cakes. They offer numerous flavors of ice cream. It is near the Piazza Teatro Massimo.

If you are near the Duomo you may try the Caffe' del Duomo, Plazza Duomo 11, Catania 95121. Tel. 095 71 50556. This café has excellent views of the Duomo and the plaza with the elefant. There are also outside tables for sitting and relaxing in the evening. Pastries, wine, and coffee are available. Inside, the meals are mostly served buffet style. In this block along the plaza there is another café with outdoor tables and you will also find a souvenir shop. The fish market is nearby as well.

For shopping, I found an excellent shop just up via Etnea. It is the Fergi Tiendo, or shop at via Etnea 92, 95128 Catania. Tel 095 311562. www.fergionline.it. They specialize in leather goods at a good quality but not as expensive as Gucci. You will find handbags and purses, women's shoes, and luggage. For men there are attache' cases, computer bags, and men's hand bags. All at affordable prices. They had prices I could afford and I purchased several items. Nearby is a similar shop called the Coin and the shop Yamamay.

While shopping I would be remiss to not mention the Catania Art of Puppet making. The famous Sicilian "pupi" can be found in souvenir shops in Palermo and Catania. It is an historical craft passed down through time. Other objects to look for are lava stone crafts and painted pottery.

Near my hotel UNA I discovered a bar called Tribeca. It is on a small alley off via Etnea almost directly across from the Una. Located at Via Monte Sant Agata, 10 Catania. Tel 095 7150240. Open 7P.M. to 2A.M. Closed on Mondays. They offer beer, wine, and apperitive. They serve free samples, dishes of Sicilian food at happy hour. Next door is a good spaghetti and pasta restaurant. There is also a nightly happy hour at the UNA which includes food sample plates.

Like all good things, my journey to Sicily must come to an end. I have fond memories. In Palermo I remember the Palermo Duomo, or Cathedral, with its mixture of architectural cultures. Nearby, the Monteale Duomo is one of the great architectural treasures with its mosaics. In Marsala, wine tasting. Then on to the Southern Coast to Argentino and the Valley of the Temples. Unforgettable to see the ruins of ancient Greek and Roman Temples. Next is Catania and Mt. Etna. The Catania Duomo is the highlight with its Baroque architecture. In the plaza is the dell Elefante, the symbol of the city. Shopping is superb. The food is typically Mediterranean and contains many spices and unique flavors. The best pastries in the world! It seems that there is nothing Sicily does not have to offer for the tourist.

My final words as I depart Sicily are "Grazie e arrivederci."

The name of my travel tour group was Gate 1 Travel, 455 Maryland Drive, Fort Washington PA. 19034. 1-800-682-3333.

6

Beijing to Moscow: The Trans-Siberian Railway

"No matter how far we travel, the memories
will follow in the baggage car."
—August Strindberg

I took a tour package with Sundowners, an Australian Company. My tour on the Trans-Siberian Railway started in Beijing, took me through Mongolia, into Siberia to see Lake Baikal, Irkutsk, Yekaterinburg, then to Moscow, and finally into St. Petersburg. Sundowners was a good value for the money. The guide was exceptional and had lots of experience on this route. He made sure we did not miss anything. It was a journey of a lifetime.

My trip started in Beijing. The must-see places are: the Great Wall, Tiananmen Square, and Chairman Mao's Mausoleum. I also highly recommend a duck dinner at a local restaurant

From Beijing we started our Trans-Mongolian, Trans-Siberian train journey. We journeyed north toward Mongolia. At the Mongolia-China border, we made a train car change because of the gauge width of the rails—we needed to change from the Chinese gauge to the Russian gauge. Passengers stepped outside to watch. Each train carriage was craned off one rail gauge and placed on the other rail gauge. The need for doing this dates back to age-old rivalries between China and Russia. After it was complete, the passengers reentered the train. Four passengers shared the train compartment. I shared my compartment with a man from the UK who was newly divorced, a college student from the UK, and the guide. There was ample room for luggage storage. We all seemed to get along well.

Originally the idea was to keep rotating the group. In the first rotation, two women from Sweden shared our cabin car, but it did not work out. I preferred to open the window for fresh air and they disagreed. Therefore, we went back to the old system for the remainder of the trip.

The focal point of the train trip was the dining car. There we could meet and greet fellow travelers as well as take our meals and drinks. In the dining car, I could sit and write my notes while watching the countryside go by. The food was reasonably good; it was always safe to order steak. There was one western-style toilet, or loo, in each train car for the passengers of the car. When I lifted the seat, I could see the tracks below. When the train stopped, the toilets were locked. On one occasion, we were on a sidetrack for six hours. I recommend bringing some extra toilet paper just in case.

Each car has an attendant, usually a lady who has her own cabin. She maintains the train car as the trip progresses. The attendant can advise you of how long a stop is, so if you leave the car, you can plan to be aboard on time and not be left behind on the platform. Stops are the perfect time to buy some snacks and drinks.

When crossing the border from Mongolia to Russia, the Russian inspectors boarded the train and checked the passports. They also searched each cabin for smuggled contraband. It was a reminder of the old communist days.

One evening, while in the dining car, I had an interesting cultural encounter. A Russian military captain sat down across from me and wanted to converse. We related the best we could given the language differences. The soldier was on vacation. He decided he wanted to prove he could drink more vodka than I could. I was game to try and make a new friend. After all, he was buying. We competed—round after round of vodka—and it did not take long for me to concede that he could outdrink me. I told him it had been a pleasure to meet him and then went to my cabin to sleep.

Later, as I was sleeping, there was a knock at our cabin door. I arose, opened the door, and found the Russian captain standing there holding a new bottle of vodka. He said, "We drink vodka!"

I responded, "No more vodka."

Then, luckily for me, one of my cabin mates, a young British man, said, "I will drink vodka with him." In relief, I sent them to the dining car to drink vodka. I went back to sleep. Never try to outdrink a Russian soldier!

In Mongolia, we crossed the steppe and came close to the Gobi. One of the highlights of Mongolia was to visit a *ger*, a traditional Mongolian nomad tent. The nomads value their homes and raise sheep, cows or yaks, goats, and camels. The camels in the Gobi are Bactrian camels and have two humps. We had an opportunity to taste alcohol made from the milk of the horse when we visited a ger.

From Mongolia, the train continued west. We reached Siberia, and our next stop was Irkutsk, which they call the Paris of Siberia. Our next visit, by tour bus, was Lake Baikal, "the Pearl of Siberia." It is the deepest lake in the world. The lake is very clear with blue, icy waters. Despite the cold, many in our group went for a short swim because the legend is a swim in Lake Baikal will add two years to one's lifespan.

From Irkutsk, we continued our train journey into Russia. Our next major city was Ekatarburg. To get there, we crossed the Ob River and traveled through Omsk. Ekatenburg was founded by Peter the Great in 1723. It is said that the Romanov family was murdered there. Next we crossed the Ural Mountains. The Urals separate Asia from Europe. We push east until we arrived in Moscow. After sightseeing, we took the night train to St. Petersburg, where the train journey ended.

St. Petersburg has become one of my favorite cities because of its rich history and magnificent architecture. Of special interest is the Hermitage Museum, one of the largest and oldest in the world. The museum has some three million objects and the largest painting collection in the world. It is also known as the Winter Palace.

The city of St. Petersburg was founded in 1703 by Tsar Peter the Great. At one time it was the capital of Russia. Peter the Great wanted Russia to become Western. St. Petersburg was to become his "window on the West." It became an important seaport on the Baltic Sea. The city has a canal system similar to Amsterdam's.

It was fitting to end our rail journey in St. Petersburg because it was the home of the first Russian railway, built in 1837. There is an excellent railway museum for train enthusiasts.

The city was named Leningrad from 1924 to 1991. Leningrad was besieged by German forces in World War II. More than a million people perished in the siege. Lenin named Leningrad one of the "Hero Cities" of the war in 1945. The city will always be remembered for its heroic resistance to the German Army. Leningrad had to be reconstructed after World War II. In 1991, it was renamed St. Petersburg.

St. Petersburg does not disappoint the visitor. It has it all—history, museums, ballet, and architecture can all be found here. It is an excellent place to start or end a Trans-Siberian Railway journey.

7

Antigua and Barbuda. Land of Sun and Sea

> "You can travel the world and never leave your
> chair when you read a book."
> —Sherry K. Plummer

The auto license plate in Antigua describes the two islands as the Island of Sun and Sea. The people are proud of their island beaches. In fact, they have over 365 beaches, one beach for each day as they proudly say. Not every beach is the same. If you search for your image of the perfect Caribbean Island then you have found it in Antigua. There is an abundance of stunning white sand beaches. It is easy to fall in love with this island. Life in Antigua revolves around the beautiful turquoise water. It is a haven for sun worshipers, snorkeling, diving, and sail boat enthusiasts.

The most recent campaign of the Antigua and Barbuda tourist offices promotes the phrase "a dream vacation where the beach is just the beginning." The beaches are the attraction but there is much culture and history to explore.

How do you travel to Antigua and Barbuda? My best choice from Atlanta was American Airlines (800-247-9297) via Miami. Most travelers wherever your trip originates will transfer in Miami. I suggest you use Kayak.com or

Farecompare.com to get your best price. Remember if it is the summer or fall, it is hurricane season. Antigua is a leeward island which means there is a chance a hurricane can postpone your trip. I suggest trip insurance to be safe during hurricane season. You can get your money back and go to Antigua at a later date. All will not be lost. This happened to me. I had to reschedule. Antigua in the Leeward islands are located right in the heart of the Caribbean. They appear on the map to "jut out" from the Caribbean into the South Atlantic.

The airport in Antigua is the V.C. Bird International Airport. The airport was named for the first prime minister of Antigua. The airport is located near the Capital, St. John's City. V.C. Bird airport is on the Northeastern end of the island. The taxi fee from V.C. Bird to St. John's is about eleven dollars US, or twenty nine dollars EC. My taxi to my hotel, Anchorage Inn, was twenty dollars. The size of Antigua is 108 square miles. The population of Antigua is about 68,000.

Barbuda has a population of 1500 people and it is located 27 miles North from Antigua. Barbuda is 62 square miles in size. You can reach Barbuda by daily ferry boat or small airplane.

My hotel choice in Antigua was the Anchorage Inn, P.O. Box 249, Anchorage Road, St. John's. Tel 268-462-4065. Fax 268-462-4066. Email info@antiguaanchorageinn. com The hotel has 40 rooms. It is a short distance from Dickerson Bay. Next door is the largest supermarket in Antigua, First Choice.

My room price was 90 US dollars, the off-season rate for a single. I was very pleased with the Anchorage Inn and its staff. The location was not on the beach but the beach was nearby the hotel. The room was upstairs with a balcony overlooking the pool, bar, and restaurant. The room had A/C, internet, ceiling fans, and cable television. I plan to return to the Anchorage Inn.

On some nights they have live Caribbean bands at the Anchorage Inn. In late April and early May, Antigua is a host to a music festival. Party people such as Jazzie B. flock here to hear the sounds of reggae island music. You will find many people from the UK to experience the music event.

The annual "Sailing Week" occurs about the same time in April. Yachts from worldwide arrive and drop anchor in English harbor. It is the most famous yacht racing event in the Caribbean. The crews compete for six days. The sight of the many colorful sails is awe inspiring. For more information visit www.sailingweek.com.

It was convenient having the first choice supermarket next door to my hotel. First choice had all the makings for sandwiches in the room and better prices especially for meat and shrimp. They have a variety of beer and wine. Basically it has everything you will find in a supermarket. It is similar to a WalMart super market. You can even find cakes, pastries, salads, pizza, cold cuts, and rotisserie chicken. Most of the items are imported from the United States. First Choice is open seven days a week from 8a.m. to 10p.m. The address for First Choice is Antigua Road, St. Johns, Antigua. Tel 1- (268) 463-3663. All the locals know it well.

The other hotels I considered were the Admirals Inn at Nelson's Dockyard at English Harbour. The hotel has only 13 rooms. The historic setting and view is tranquil and informal. The historic feel appeals to many tourists. It has A/C and ceiling fans. The restaurant is excellent. The address is PO Box 713, St. John's. Tel (268) 460-1027/1153. Fax (268) 460-1534. Email www.admiralsantigua.com.

Looking for an all-inclusive directly on the beach? I recommend Halcyon Rex Resort on Dickenson Bay. There are 226 rooms on perhaps the most beautiful beach in Antigua. Tel (268) 462-0258, Fax (268) 462-0271. Email rexhalcyon@candw.ag.

The beach at Dickenson Bay is a short distance from my hotel, The Anchorage Inn. A taxi is available also. At the end of the street you see the beach. There you will find Tony's Beach Bar and Restaurant. Tony's also has watersports and can book fishing trips. It is your typical local beach bar locally owned and run by Tony. Rum punch is his specialty. Tony's also has an excellent kitchen and serves a daily lunch of local cuisine. Locals flock there to get a carry-out lunch. Favorite dishes are barbecue chicken or fish. Also you can have pepper pot soup made with dumplings, a classic Antiguan dish. The soup is made from parts of a pig, cow, or chicken is often served. Ducana, a sweet potato dumpling, is popular. Besides rum drinks there are the local beers such as Wadadli and Carib. Don't miss a trip to Tony's. Tony's phone number is 462-6326. Email is Tonyswatersports@hotmail.com. Located on the beach at Dickenson Bay St. Johns Antigua. Meals range from 5.00 to 10.00 ECUs.

If you walk to the North on the beach you will come to the Halcyon Rex Beach Resort on Dickenson Bay. This is a 226 room all inclusive resort with beautifully landscaped grounds. Rooms go from $125.00 and higher. The Arawak Terrace is the well-known restaurant of the Halcyon. It is noted for serving a delicious Creole buffet.

Walking South from Tony's, you pass the Sandals Grande Antigua. Sandals has nine restaurants and the largest pool in Antigua. Sandals appeals to couples in search of unforgettable romance.

Continue walking on the beach and you will next arrive at the Coconut Grove Restaurant and Bar. It is located next to the Siboney Beach Club, Dickenson Bay. 268-462-1538. The Coconut Grove is a classic Caribbean restaurant and bar located right on the beach with a thatch roof.

The Coconut Grove is now owned by a Danish person, Johnny Tved. The owner, while on vacation, fell in love with Antigua and the Coconut Grove. He made an offer and the offer was accepted.

The Coconut Grove is somewhat upscale compared to Tony's and is open in the evenings. The email is www.coco nutgroveantigua.com. Tel. 462-1538. It is open from 7:30am-11pm daily. Service is excellent. Great view! Owner on premises. The London Times describes the Coconut Grove "Every visitors dream of what a Caribbean beach bar and restaurant should be." Some examples from the Coconut Grove menu are:

Two eggs .... EC 26.00
Pancakes.. EC 20.00

For lunch you can have:

Calamari .... EC 32.00
BBQ wings EC35.00

and my favorite

Fish Burger .... EC 36.00
Regular hamburger .... EC 36.00
Bread pudding .... EC 30.00
Salt fish .... EC 32.00
Catch of the day...................................... EC 76.00

Seafood Pasta .... EC 65.00
Rock Lobster .... EC 98.00
Old English Rum .... EC 25.00
Pina Colada .... EC 12.00

They have an outstanding selection of wines from France, Italy, and Spain.

The official currency of Antigua is the EC, or Eastern Caribbean dollar. The exchange rate is US 1.00 = EC 2.65. Major credit cards are taken. Tipping on Antigua is at 10-15% depending on the service. Sometimes 10% tip is automatically added. You will have to ask.

Pepper pot soup or stew is most popular not only in Antigua but throughout the West Indies. You can also find it today in Philadelphia, USA. The story is that George Washington brought the soup to the colonies and it became popular. In 1751, Washington visited his brother in Barbados where he first had the soup. Washington brought the recipe back to the colonies.

At Valley Forge, during the harsh winter, Washington served a version of the soup to his starving and freezing troops. The soup may have played a role in the victory in the Revolutionary War.

No visit to Antigua is complete without a visit to the restaurant PaPa Zouk, located at Hilda Davis Dr. in a neighborhood near St. John's. 268-464-6044. The locals love it as well. If you like seafood, especially fish, it is a must. Also they are known for their rum punch.

The sign out front reads "Papa Zouk Fish and Rum. Great fish, largest selection of rums and Zouk music." Now you are in the Island spirit.

It is a small and cozy place. I visited at night and sat outside under the canopy to stay cool. I had a variety of grilled fish samples, rice, beans, and salad. Of course, I had the rum punch. Very tasty and satisfying. Service was excellent.

The grilled snapper is about 20 USD. Main courses are 20 USD-28 USD. Be sure to meet Faye, the owner. It is the best local restaurant on Antigua.

Another excellent restaurant featuring local food is the Hummingbird Restaurant and Bar affiliated with the Anchorage Inn, where I stayed in Antigua. The restaurant and bar are located in the back of the Inn in a patio setting next to the pool. The manager and chief chef is Nigel. Nigel is friendly and personable. Nigel is also a good source of island information. He loves to please his customers. His motto is "Food that makes you go Hummm!

The menu is varied. Nigel is a local and can prepare for you almost anything. Just say "I want what the locals eat." He can do it. For example, corn and sweet potatoes are popular dishes. Otherwise, some choices are:

BBQ Chicken .... EC 10.00
Fish Burger .... EC 8.00
Salads .... EC 8.00-10.00

Excellent rum punch. The local dishes come with the sides of rice and beans.

In addition

Grouper .... EC 21.00
Steak .... EC 21.00
Lobster Tail .... EC 28.00

Frequently bands appear at night on the patio by the pool. I saw a fabulous local group called "Three Cylinders."

They play island reggae and other international songs. My favorite was "We came from a land down under!" Great rendition and extra volume.

Shopping is always a vital part of travel. I love to bring home something meaningful such as a piece of art or something to represent the culture.

I was excited to discover in English Harbor a gallery named, Things Local. It is housed in the former officers quarters built by Admiral Nelson in the Dockyards. A quaint, wooden building. Most of the works of art in the gallery are the work of Carl Henry, who is one of Antigua's best wood carvers. Mr. Henry happened to be in the shop on the day I visited. I purchased from him a carving of a sea turtle. He said it was an off day and he was willing to bargain. Never be afraid to ask for a discount even if you are speaking with a famous artist. I highly recommend this shop when visiting historic Nelson's Dockyard. It is located just to the right as you enter the gates.

Another favorite art shop of mine is The Pottery Shop located on Redcliffe Quay, St. John's town. Tel 1-268-462-5503. This is the best place for buying vases and plates. The work is very colorful and make great gifts for the friends back home.

Pottery making in Antigua dates back to the Amerindians. Be sure to stop by the pottery shop to enjoy the vibrant colors of the pottery made from Antiguan clay. Sarah Fuller is perhaps the best known pottery artist in Antigua. Visit www.sarahfullerpottery.com.

Now a word about the historical roots of Antigua. The first settlers were the Arawak Indians. In 35 AD to 1100 AD. They were followed by the Carib people, hence the name Caribbean.

The first European to discover Antigua was Christopher Columbus in 1493. Columbus did not make land but gave the island its name. Columbus named it for a Spanish Saint, Santa Maria la Antigua.

The English arrived in 1632. The most famous was Sir Christopher Codrington who came from Barbados to establish sugarcane growing as the cash crop.

Horatio Nelson, Senior British Naval officer, arrived in Antigua to establish in 1785 a base for England's sea power in the Caribbean. His job was to enforce trade laws. Nelson's Dockyard is named for him. The Dockyard once housed British Naval officers and English harbor was the colonial base for the Royal Navy. Today, English Harbor is the focal point for international sailing and yachting.

Sugarcane plantations brought slaves from Africa. Finally in 1834, England abolished slavery. Today tourism and finance are the major sources of income. The port is also a source of commerce and trade.

Antigua gained independence from the English in 1981. Vere Cornwall Bird became the Prime Minister. The government is a parliamentary democracy and a member of the Commonwealth of Nations.

Nelson's Dockyard in English Harbor is a major historical attraction for tourists. After paying a small entrance fee, one can walk around to soak in the history. Tourists are free to explore the old buildings. There is a museum and visitor's center. It is a great place for lunch with many restaurants and cafes. My favorite place to dine is the Copper and Lumber Store restaurant and hotel. The Admiral's Inn is another combination hotel and restaurant. It was built in 1788. It is constructed of brick brought from England.

The entrance fee to Nelson's Dockyard includes access to Shirley Heights. It is the highest point in Antigua. Originally it was designed as a fortification with canons and barracks overlooking the ocean. There is an unforgettable panoramic view. A must photo stop.

Betty's Hope is yet another historical site. It was built in 1674 by Sir Christopher Codrington. It was the first full-scale sugar plantation.

Back in St. Johns is the St. John's Cathedral. It was first built in 1681. Later it was rebuilt with stone. At the top of the hill, it can be seen from St. John's town below. The church is Anglican. The interior is a must see. Just follow Temple Street North.

While in St. John's town, be sure to stop by the local artisans market to bargain for arts and crafts. It is located Recliffe and St. Mary's streets. I bought a small colorful painting for 15 USD. Gamblers will enjoy King's Casino. It is located in the heart of St. John's in Heritage Quay. They offer 21 Black Jack, Roulette, Stud Poker, and slot machines. You can watch and wager on your favorite sports teams. Also, there is simulcast horse or dog racing.

We cannot leave Antigua without at least a day trip to Barbuda. This island is part of Antigua, the sister island. The population is about 1600. Most live in the town of Codrington. It is known for its beautiful pink and white beaches. It is a touch of paradise.

The best way to travel to Barbuda is by the daily ferry from Heritage Quay in St. John's. The other option is by small plane owned by Montserrant Air. Their number is 268-562-7183 in Antigua.

The Barbuda Express Ferry seats fifty six passengers. It will cost EC 220 round trip. Make sure you take sea sickness pills. It takes about ninety minutes. The ferry leaves from Point Warf in St. John's. Tel 268-560-7989.

There are only two hotels in Barbuda. They are Coco Point Lodge and the Lighthouse Bay Resort.

Coco Point has thirty-five rooms and is made up of beach cottages or villas. It is located on a beautiful pink and white beach. It includes an excellent restaurant. Water sports and fishing are available. The managers are a husband and wife team, Ray and Danielle. The atmosphere is low key and intimate. Coco Point is considered pricey. It is all inclusive, and the service and staff are excellent. A single room is 900 USD and a double is 1200 USD. But the rate includes transportation and meals with beverages. Tel. 268-462-3816. reservations@cocopoint.com.

The Lighthouse Bay Resort is even more pricey than Coco Point. The price is from 1,630 USD. Expect to pay 40 USD for a rum punch at the bar. What draws people there is its spectacular location. It faces the Caribbean Sea looking west and a shallow lagoon to the east. They pride themselves on their gourmet chef and excellent service by the staff. The address is 1 Lighthouse Bay Resort, Codrington. Antigua and Barbuda. 1-888-214-8552 or 268-562-1481. www.lighthousebayresort.com.

If you take a day trip to Barbuda, be sure to see the Frigate Bird Sanctuary. It is the largest in the world. Of course you will enjoy the twelve miles of pink and white sand beaches.

Life in Antigua and Barbuda revolves around the ocean. There are plenty of beaches for being active or relaxing in a hammock with a rum punch. You can swim, snorkel, scuba, or go sailing.

"The beach is just the beginning" as they say in Antigua. There is much history and culture. Visit Nelson's

Harbour, Old Sugar Mills, Shirley Heights, or go shopping. Go dining and have the lobster or snapper. Try the local creole dishes. The choices are many.

Expedia voted Antigua and Barbuda "The best beach destination in the World." Enjoy!

8

Yucatán, Mexico: The Mayan Empire

"How beautiful it is to do nothing and
then rest afterwards."
—Spanish Proverb

Over the years, I have made numerous trips to the
Yucatán. It is one of my favorite destinations. I
especially enjoy Playa del Carmen. I make Playa my home
base when I'm in the Yucatán, sometimes called the Mexican
Riviera. Playa is less crowded and less glitzy than Cancún.
The beaches are very sandy, and the surf is not as difficult.
Cozumel is a short ferry ride away. Playa was once a small
fishing village. It is also the gateway to the Mayan pyramids
of Tulum and Coba, both a short bus ride away.

To get to Playa from the Cancún airport, simply take
either the bus or a taxi. Playa is sixty miles south of Cancún.
There are many budget hotels in Playa. My favorite two
are Hotel Plaza and Hotel Colibri. Prices range from fifty
to sixty dollars. The Colibri is directly on the beach and
has a dive center. The Plaza Hotel is across the street. Both
are convenient to the beach and downtown fifth avenue.
The El Pirata Beach Bar and Restaurant is across the street
from the Plaza. It has great margaritas. Less than an hour

south of Playa is Tulum, the site of a pre-Columbian Mayan pyramid, called El Castillo. Tulum today is a popular site for tourists.

Tulum is the only Mayan city built directly on the ocean. It is located on a bluff overlooking the Caribbean Sea. Tulum dates from AD 400 to AD 900 and is one of the best-preserved Mayan sites. After exploring the Mayan ruins, many people go swimming from the beautiful beach located below the ruins. Many spend the night in one of Tulum's many tourist hotels, such as Cabanas.

Some tourists continue south of Tulum to Punta Allen. If nothing else, this makes a good day trip to the Sian Ka'an Biosphere Reserve to get away from civilization and to go snorkeling. You can view sea turtles and dolphins. Also, there is bird watching. Finish the day with grilled fish in the small village of Punta Allen.

Next, take a day trip to the Mayan ruins at Coba, about thirty minutes west of Tulum. You can rent a car or take a bus. There is a small village at Coba, featuring restaurants that serve local dishes.

Coba is in the middle of a jungle and offers a different experience. You may perhaps see or hear howler monkeys. Coba is located near two lagoons and contains several large pyramids. The tallest pyramid is called Nohoch Mul. Tourists are allowed to climb the pyramid's 120 steps. From the top, there is a panoramic view of the jungle and the lake.

The best-known and most popular Mayan pyramid is Chichen Itza. To get there from Playa, it is a three-hour ride via Cancún. The pyramid known as El Castillo, one of the New Seven Wonders of the World, is the tallest. In an effort to preserve the stones, the public is no longer allowed to climb it.

Be sure to visit the ballgame court. It is said that the losers of a ballgame were executed.

A day trip to the colonial city of Valladolid is recommended to view the colonial architecture and culture of old Mexico. Merida is another example of a colonial town.

Back in Playa, another option is to take the short ferry ride to Cozumel. Many tour ships make port in Cozumel. It is also an ideal place to dive or snorkel to see the famous Palancar Reef.

As you can see, Playa del Carmen makes the ideal base for your travels throughout the Yucatán. Make sure you take time to enjoy the beaches and crystal clear waters of the Caribbean.

9

Merida. The Land of the Maya

"Twenty years from now you will be
more disappointed by the things you
didn't do than by the ones you did do.
So throw off the bow lines, sail
away from the safe harbor. Catch
the trade winds in your sails.
Explore. Dream. Discover.
—Mark Twain

Merida was my travel base in the ancient land of the Maya in the Yucatan, Mexico. I arrived in the Cancun Airport. From the terminal I boarded the Ado bus for a four-hour ride to Merida. The bus is a first class bus with toilet and air conditioning. The single ticket was about 40 USD.

The view from the bus was almost boring. On each side one could see the dense jungle passing by. In May the climate was hot and humid. It is necessary to stay hydrated. The land is flat. Merida has a population of about 710,000 and is a melting pot of Hispanic and indigenous cultures such as the Maya.

Pre-Hispanic Merida was founded in the 13th century AD. It was originally a Mayan City named, Tho. The Spanish, under Francisco de Montejo, arrived in 1526. His son completed the founding of the city and he gave it the name Merida in 1542.

My hotel selection in Merida was the charming and historical Hotel Dolores Alba. The Alba is located just off the heart of the historic district at Calle 63 No 464 x 52 y54. Merida Yucatan Mexico 97000. Tel 999 928 5650. Toll free 01-888-849-50-60. Email@doloresalba.com. It is like an oasis in the city with a swimming pool and tropical plants. The lobby contains historic artifacts. The lobby resembles a hacienda of the Spanish Colonial style.

The room rate for a single at the Alba is 46 USD. The rooms are clean and have air conditioning. There is daily maid service. A free breakfast is included.

The Dolores Alba has a branch hotel in Chichen Itza. The desk personnel can arrange a transfer for you. It is a short distance from the El Castillo pyramid. It is also 122 km on the free road from Cancun if you are driving. Tel 01 985 808 55 56 and 88 15 55.

For those who prefer a hostel to save money, I recommend the Hostel Zocalo located in Calle 63 adjacent to Casa de Montejo. Take the side entrance and climb the stairs. Some rooms have balconies overlooking the south side of the Grand Plaza, or the main square. Single room rates are 30 USD, or try bargaining for a better room rate. The address is Hostel Zocalo, Calle 63 entre 60 and 62, #508 Merida, Mexico Yucatan 97000. The Hostel advertises "A hostel with the feel of a guest house."

The main square, or Zocalo, is the focal point of the historical district of Merida. The Plaza is bordered by Calle

60, 61, 62, and 63. It is a popular gathering spot day or night.

My favorite restaurant and sidewalk café is the La Via Olimpo, the Restaurant, Bar, and Café. This café is located in the historic Palacio Municipal, or City Government Building. The owner and manager is Ma. Victoria Sivilla Ruiz and her son Chris. Victoria is on the premises during the day. She is a pleasant woman to speak with and gain tourist information.

The address of La Via is Calle 62 No. 502 Depto, 2 x 61 y 63 cal. Centro. CP 97000 Merida, Yucatan, Mexico. Tel 999 923 58 43. Located directly across from the Zocalo de Merida in the center of the historical district. The morning coffee and pastry crowd is interesting. It is populated by mostly retired Mexican men discussing politics and world affairs. The operating hours are from 7:00 am to 11:00 pm.

I took some notes from the menu of LaVia. Some examples are:

Continental Breakfast ....48 pesos
Café ....18 pesos
Water or Agua..20 pesos

For lunch and dinner

Enchiladas...125 pesos
Fajitas..95 pesos
Meats...140 pesos
Hamburger ....65 pesos
Beer ....26 pesos
Wine..49 pesos
Cola...20 pesos

The prices are moderate but the food and service is excellent. Be sure to say hello to Victoria and Chris.

Another restaurant I recommend is the LaParrila, one block off the Centro, or Zocalo. Turn off Calle 61 onto Calle 60, near the Cathedral. Tel 928 16 91. LaParilla is a Mexican chain. There is a LaParilla in Playa Carmen. It is noted for its grilled food such as fresh fish, steak, and lobster.

If you want to experience a strictly local beer bar, try P.P. Lopez which is popular with workers for drinking cheap beer and listening to Ranchero Music. It is located almost adjacent to the Hotel Dolores Alba on Calle 63. Beer is only 20 pesos and they offer all the popular brands such as Sol, Dos XX, and Corona. My favorite Mexican beer is Bohemia. Sometimes I like Superior or Pacifico.

For shopping there are numerous shops for souvenirs and artifacts scattered around the Grand Plaza or Zocalo. Always bargain.

The Presuel artisans shop next to the Cathedral is a favorite of mine. They offer many traditional items such as the famous Guayaberas Yucatan Shirt made of cotton or linen. The price can range from 35 to 50 USD. The address is Calle 61 no. 501 entre 60 y 62. Merida Yucatan Mexico CP97000. Tel 999 928 2622.

The shop Guayaberas Yucatan specializes only in the Guayaberas shirt. It also has the famous Yucatan hammocks and the popular Panama hats. It is located at Calle 63-A No 519 Int 4. Merida Yucatan Mexico. Tel 252 73 01. Email escobar2376@hotmail.com. They are a distributor and ship worldwide.

My favorite book store in Merida is Librerias Danti, or Dante. Dante is also a publisher of books. They are located next to LaVia Café across from the Zocalo on Calle

62 Centro. Tel 9 28 36 74. They have other locations in Merida and Mexico. It is fun to browse through the books, especially the literature and history books written in both Spanish and English. They also have maps and school books.

There are many taxis in Merida making it easy and economical to move about. I used Taxis Santa Fe most often. They provide excellent 24-hour service. Tel 924 59 18.

The best way to tour the city of Merida is to take the 'Get On and Get Off' red tourist bus. It departs in the Zocalo almost directly across from the cathedral. It takes about an hour and half to cover the historic route.

Paseo de Montejo is often called the "Champs Elysees" of Merida. If you enjoy colonial homes and museums, then you need a stroll up Paseo de Montejo extending out from Calle 60 starting at the Zocalo. There are beautiful palaces and Mansions to see. Some of the mansions have been abandoned and left in disrepair. The horse drawn carriages are another way to see the Paseo.

Be sure to visit the Museum of Anthropology at the corner of Calle 43. The museum is housed in the historic mansion Palacio Canton. It was the home of General Francisco Canton Rosado. It was constructed between 1904 and 1911. My impression is that the exhibits focus on numerous excavations in the Yucatan such as Chichen Itza. There are various old photographs and some stone carvings. It is worth the visit. There is a small gift shop on the way out. I purchased a DVD which looks at all the major excavations of the Maya Pyramids. The address is Paseo Montejo and Calle 43.

Be sure to visit Montejo's House. It is a free entry fee. It was built by Francisco Montejo in 1543 in the architectural style of Spanish Colonial. The house is located on Calle

63 facing the Zocalo, or main Plaza. The son of Montejo inherited the house. Inside you can see the typical furniture of the period and imagine how a typical royal family lived. Today it is considered a national heritage.

No visit to Merida is complete without a visit to the Merida Cathedral of San Ildefonso. Construction began in 1561 and completed in 1598. The stones used to build the cathedral came from the Maya buildings destroyed by the Spanish. It is constructed in Renaissance style with medieval and Moorish influences. The outside has what some call a "fortress like" appearance. The doorway is called the "forgiveness" doorway. The cathedral opens in the afternoon at 4pm. Be sure to see the carved wooden cross which is the largest cross carved from wood in the Americas.

My next stop was a day trip from Merida to the ancient Maya city of Uxmal and the Grand Pyramid of the Magician, on the Sorcerer's Pyramid. Uxmal dates from between the 7th and 10th centuries AD. The first Mayans actually arrived about 500 BC. At its high point of civilization, the area had 25,000 occupants.

The Sorcerer's Pyramid is named, according to Maya mythology, when an old woman witch found an egg. When the egg hatched a young boy sprang out. The boy grew no larger than a dwarf. He eventually became the ruler and in a single night, constructed the 115 ft. pyramid. However it was built, it is the most impressive Maya Pyramid I have seen.

It took me two hours to tour the Uxmal ruins. Behind the main pyramid is the Birds' Quadrangle. You will find ornamental bird motifs on the walls. Next is the Nuns' Quadrangle. It is called the Nunnery because it resembles a Spanish convent.

Opposite the Nunnery is the Ball Court. Practically all Maya cities have a ball court. The ball game was played with rubber spheres, or balls. The players had to keep the ball moving and to score by sending it through one of two stone rings. Mythology has it that the losing team were sacrificed as a part of a religious ritual. The teams literally played their hearts out.

The Iguana building comes next. The house of the Iguana consists of eleven columns. It was an administrative building. Another important building is the Governor's Palace. Notice the typical Mayan arch in the detail of the Dovecote building. In front of the Governor's Palace is the two-headed Jaguar stone carving. The jaguar is held in reverence in the Yucatan and Central America.

A visit to Uxmal leaves a lasting impression upon the visitor. The Pyramid of the Magician dominates this Maya city. Uxmal, with its layout of beautiful buildings decorated with mosaics, is an outstanding example of Maya architecture. The memory of Uxmal will sustain itself in your memory.

Back in Merida, I prepare for my departure to Cancun. I take a taxi to the bus station, CAME, on Calle 70. The ADO bus to Cancun travels from here. Tickets can be purchased at the bus station.

As I depart Merida I reflect back on my Maya adventure. Merida is a wonderful colonial city, well worth the visit. It is full of history, museums, and beautiful architecture. I enjoyed walking the streets, park benches, and cafes with the people watching, or the passing parade. The people are friendly. There is enough to do and see to keep you busy for a week.

Uxmal made a lasting impression. It is one of the best examples of Maya architecture. There are hundreds of Maya historical sites in the Yucatan. It could take years to visit them all. Therefore, I recommend visiting Uxmal, Chichen Itza, Tulum, and Coba in Mexico. Tikal in Guatemala. Your budget and time will be a factor in your choices. Whatever your choices, we will continue to be fascinated by the Maya civilization.

"The blood of the chieftains ran like water." Thomas, The Conquest of Mexico. p 390.

Maya Timeline of Mesoamerica

3000-1500 BC	Migration across the Bering Strait
1500 BC-100 AD	Preclassic. Maya villages developed in lowlands Yucatan
500 BC	Uxmal founded
250 BC-1000	Classic Period. Tikal founded in Guatemala. Tikal was one of the largest Maya cities. Mayas spread into Mexico.
435 AD	Chichen Itza. El Castillo Regional Maya capital of Yucatan. Religious and political center. Discoveries in Mathematics, astrology, and hieroglyphics.
500-900 AD	Coba. Classic period. Nohoch Mul pyramid. Agriculture.
1325 AD	Tennochtitlan. Aztec city in Valley of Mexico. Pyramids of Sun and Moon. Military giant late 1400's.
900-1540 AD	Tulum. Post Classic. The pyramid El Castillo overlooks the Caribbean. Major trade depot.

| 1519 | Cortez and the Spanish conquest. Clash of civilizations. |
| 1520 | Death of Montezuma II |

Maya Yucatan History

Pre classical 1500-150 BC. The Olmec and Maya. Mesoamerica culture. Agriculture.

Classical. 150-925 BC. Pyramid building. Maya concept of zero. Agriculture flourished.

Post Classical. 925 BC to 1530 AD. Toltec influence on Maya. The demist of the Maya.

Cortez arrives 1519. The Spanish conquest of the Maya and the Aztec.

10

Cancun. Mexico's Party Capital

One's destination is never a place
but a new way of seeing things.
—Henry Miller

Cancun is a modern beachside metropolis similar to Miami, USA. It does not resemble the authentic Mexican culture of the Maya. There are numerous multistory hotels with glitz and glamor. If you are looking for comfort, sun bathing, water sports, and fine dining you will find it in Cancun. The prices are higher as well. I found Cancun to be a comfortable place to stay for a few days after my tour of Merida and the Maya structures before my air trip back home. Although at times I thought I was already in the USA since there were shopping malls, McDonalds, Subway, and the Outback Restaurants. It is your choice.

For convenience and relaxation, I selected the all-inclusive Barcelo Tucancun Beach Resort. This Barcelo is located at Avenida Kukulcan, 77500 Cancun Q Roo. Tel No +52 998 8915900. Toll free 1-800-227-2356. You can also use their App. at myBarcelo. Fax +52 998 8850615. Email tucancun@barcelo.com. My single room facing the ocean was priced at 104 USD. Very reasonable for the inclusion rate with meals, drinks, and activities. This is the advantage of an all-inclusive hotel. Also, there is nightly live entertainment.

You can reach the hotel by taxi from either the Cancun Airport or the downtown central Cancun bus terminal. From the airport, head north. You will reach the Kukulkan Ave. Then continue until you see the hotel which is located on the right. It is about 25 minutes from the airport.

The official currency is the Mexican peso. The exchange rate at this time was 12.50 pesos per US dollar. But the US dollar is widely accepted throughout Mexico. ATM's are plentiful.

Often the Barcelo will offer resort credit, such as US $100.00 to use at the resort. There is a Spa on the premises and fine dining as well as a la carte. Various sports options are offered. They also have dancing lessons and Spanish language lessons. There are three swimming pools, four restaurants, and five bars. A kids club is available.

The Barcelo is located on a beautiful white sandy beach. The Mexican Caribbean Ocean has exceptionally clean turquoise waters.

Shopping is nearby and easily available. Prices tend to be higher than found in Merida, Playa Carmen, or Tulum. But you have many choices. A short taxi ride away you can find the souvenir warehouse. Everything Mexico, it contains souvenirs from all over Mexico. Prices are reasonable but there is no bargaining.

You can find mercados or markets for bargaining in Cancun such as Mercado 23, Mercado 28, or where Cancun and Xcaret meet. The markets offer artisans or popular handicrafts made from silver, copper, ceramics, leather, and colorful fabrics. The best item is authentic Taxco silver. The Mexicans are great silversmiths.

Shopping malls are plentiful as well. There is the Plaza Caracol, Plaza Forum, and just outside the Barcelo is Plaza Isla and Plaza Kukutan. The La Isla also contains restaurants, bars, and discos. But why go somewhere else when you have practically everything in the all-inclusive Barcelo.

If you do venture out at night, I suggest you take the party Hopper bus. You start at the Congo Bar then Senor Frogs, and end at the City at midnight. It includes entrance fees and unlimited national bar. It is priced at 65 USD.

Another reason to venture out is to visit Maya sites to learn history and about the architecture. It would be a shame to travel to Mexico and not visit historical sites. Also, it is a chance to meet the people.

Chichen Itza is the most popular Maya destination. This was a Mayan political and religious center with the impressive well preserved pyramid El Castillo. A must see.

Other places to visit are Tulum, Coba, and the beach village, Playa del Carmen. They call it the Mayan Riviera. You can rent a car or book a tour at the Barcelo desk. Such a trip will inspire the visitor to read and study about the Maya when they return home.

Xcaret will appeal to kids and the entire family. It is an ecological park with snorkeling and wild life. The Captain Hook Pirate Adventure will appeal to the kids. The trip is aboard a replica of a pirate ship. A simulated pirate attack is re-enacted.

A word about Maya food. Foods such as guacamole, tamales, chocolate, corn tortillas, chili pepper, enchiladas, corn and beans were favorite foods of the Mayas. Today the Mexican diet is a fusion of indigenous and Spanish recipes.

The proximity of the ocean makes it possible to have fresh seafood. Fresh fruit platters are also served regularly especially for breakfast. Mexico has readily available tropical fruits. The banana is popular. Many people do not realize that the Mayans first grew cocoa plants about 600 AD. The Mayas called chocolate "the drink of the Gods.' Cacao beans were used as currency. Montezuma especially enjoyed chocolate and offered cocoa as a peace offering to the Spanish invaders.

The Spanish introduced horses which eventually led to the cattle industry. The caballero culture is important in Mexican culture.

Maize (corn) in the history of Mexico.

Maize was first domesticated from a grass plant in Mexico and dates from the Mayas and Aztecs. It was developed at least 7000 years ago.

Corn became a major part of the diet in Mexico. Corn is used in making tacos, tamales, and tortillas.

Beans, or Frijoles, are part of the daily diet in Mexico. Black beans are popular in the Yucatan.

Most Mexican dishes use Chiles. The poblano is popular and can range from mild to very hot. The chipotle is also used widely in the Mexican diet.

Travelers' Health in Mexico.

The most common problem when traveling in Mexico is diarrhea, or digestive problems. Gringos sometimes refer to it as "Montezuma's revenge." Once you have diarrhea it can take three days to run its course if you are lucky.

The simple cause of diarrhea is bacteria. You need to prevent the bacteria from getting to your stomach. Wash your hands frequently. Drink purified water. Be careful with ice in your drinks or if the lettuce is washed properly. Be careful eating tacos and tamales from street vendors. The old rule is "if you can't peel it then don't eat it." You can peel bananas or an orange. Watch for flies touching your food.

Diarrhea medicine you should pack in your travel medical kit are Imodium, Pepto Bismol, and antibacterial hand wipes. But remember Imodium only stops your digestive system and does not get to the cause. Sometimes relief is preferable since you want to feel better. Dehydration can occur which means you need to drink plenty of bottled water. Gatorade can help restore your electrolytes and put the body system on balance. Antibiotics could aid the body to rid itself of bacteria.

Travel sickness is akin to diarrhea. This can come from rapid changes in your environment, such as flying long distances. Your daily routine changes. Maybe you drink too much or eat exotic foods. Your body needs to adapt. Be sure to drink plenty of bottled water. Also, watch for sunburn. Lack of sleep is another factor.

Altitude sickness when traveling to Mexico City can cause discomfort since Mexico City is over 7000 feet above sea level. Dizziness, nausea, and shortness of breath are common symptoms. Get a prescription of Diamox from your doctor to use as a prevention.

Malaria is no longer common in Mexico. If you plan to spend time in the jungle or river area, you may want to check with the CDC, or Centers for Disease Control, for advice. You can also visit a medical center which offers shots and medical advice about preventing a disease. The carriers of malaria are mosquitoes. The mosquitoes bite usually between dusk and dawn. The main symptom is a high fever accompanied by chills, sweat, headache, and body aches.

Malaria is always a serious disease. Plan to use mosquito nets when sleeping or using a bug spray with a high level of deet in its content. Wear long pants and long sleeve shirts.

An unusual health hazard can occur when swimming in the ocean. It is the jelly fish. Strong tides or winds may drive them onto beaches. The sting of the jelly fish is the cause for concern. They have long tentacles which can sting and be very painful causing red welts. Most often the sting does not cause death but it is recommended to see a doctor right away especially if the rash worsens.

The "hangover" is considered a health consideration. I write about the hangover since Cancun is the "party center." Drinking alcohol has a dehydrating effect on the body and causes headaches. A person should limit the amount of alcohol they consume. The more you drink or the more you guzzle in a short period of time, the worse the hangover.

As a remedy for a hangover is to drink water as you consume alcohol. You need to be rehydrated. Eat something simple such as eggs. Take vitamin B1 or a B vitamin complex. When you drink you deplete yourself of the B vitamins. Drink a glass of water before going to bed. Drinking gatorade can help rebuild your supply of electrolytes. The "hair of the dog" is not a remedy, it only prolongs the hangover. As Clint Eastwood once said, "A man needs to know his limits."

Sunburn can be a health hazard when on the beach or touring the Mayan ruins. Avoid over exposure to the sun since Mexico has intense sun most of the year. It is best to use sunscreen of at least SPE 15, 30, or 50 for the best skin protection. Wear a hat and a long sleeve shirt. When snorkeling, wear a T-shirt and don't forget to put sunscreen on the back of your legs.

It is best to check with the CDC and see your doctor before you travel. This way you get the vaccinations and travel medicine you will need. You will know your travel risks. Take out travel insurance. Take a first aid kit with you for an emergency. The Centers for Disease Control and Prevention (CDC) is the national public health institute of the United States. It is a federal agency. The CDC is located in Atlanta, Ga. USA. It is a good source of travel health advice. You can contact the CDC at 1-800-232-4636 or www.cdc.gov/ and www.nc.cdc.gov/travel/. The UK and European version of the CDC is the European Centre for Disease Prevention and Control in Stockholm Sweden. Contact the ECDC at www.ecdc.europa.edu/ or www.ecdc.europa.eu.

Cancun stands in contrast to some other cities such as Merida which dates back in history. But Cancun is well worth visiting if you budget and plan properly. The beach is beautiful. The nightlife and cuisine are excellent. The Mayan ruins are nearby. Cancun can be an educational experience. Mexico is an unforgettable country and its people are some of the most friendly in the hemisphere of the Americas.

11

Argentina and Uruguay: Wine and the Beach

"Travel is like knowledge. The more you see,
the more you know you haven't seen."
—Mark Hertsgaard

The wine country in Argentina is located primarily in Mendoza and the surrounding region of Cuyo. Cuyo is a mountainous area in central-western Argentina. The Aconcagua Mountain is located here. Wine production is the main economic activity. Residents also grow olive trees and some fruits.

My visit to Mendoza was the highlight of my trip. It is a beautiful Spanish colonial city with wide streets and parks. Mendoza is a nice change of pace from the hustle and bustle of Buenos Aires. It is a more tranquil, smaller city and provides a good base for visiting the wineries.

The Spanish colonials settled in Mendoza in 1561. It is about 500 miles Northwest of Buenos Aires. To travel there, I flew with LAN Chile. You can also travel by bus.

Mendoza sits at the base of the Andes Mountains, second only in height to the Himalayas. Mendoza is compact and pedestrian friendly. Also, there are buses and the trolley.

Taxis are readily available and cheap. Some people rent a bicycle while they are there.

Aconcagua is the highest peak in the Andes. Travel agents can organize trekking tours in the summer and ski trips in the winter. Bariloche is a popular ski destination in the Andes.

The Parque San Martín is nice for walking or hiking around. The Plaza Independencia in downtown Mendoza is an excellent place to explore the main square. Plaza España is the most beautiful plaza in the city, reflecting Mendoza's relationship with Spain. You will find Spanish motifs all around the Plaza and easily see the Spanish cultural heritage.

My hotel in Mendoza was the Aconcagua Hotel, named for the Andean peak and located in the heart of Mendoza, almost in the front of Plaza Italia. The address is San Lorenzo 545, 5500 Mendoza. It is a four-star hotel and the price is about one hundred to one hundred fifty US dollars.

The hotel was not far from Plaza Independencia. I booked it with my travel agent, but it can be booked independently. I liked it because of the location. The breakfast buffet was excellent. It was clean and well maintained, and the staff was friendly. There was a swimming pool as well.

Adjacent to the hotel is the restaurant Los Parrales. It offers a fusion cuisine but also offers Argentinian steaks and wine. The room is decorated with wine memorabilia. I highly recommend Los Parrales whether you stay in the hotel or not.

As in Europe, I enjoyed the sidewalk cafés. One can sit with a glass of wine or a cappuccino and pastry while watching the passing parade of people. There is no better way to get to know a country and its people.

It is easy to visit the wineries, or bodegas. Most are free to visit. The wineries are located outside Mendoza on what they call the wine roads. Mendoza wineries are the producers of the malbec wine, which is growing in worldwide popularity. This region is called the high zone because of the elevation. The Mendoza East region also produces malbec wine. Malbec is produced in the Cuyo valley and regions south of Mendoza South regions.

Malbec today is the most widely planted red-grape variety in Argentina. The first malbec vines came to Argentina from France in the mid-nineteenth century. Akin to a cabernet sauvignon, malbec is pleasant; it has a medium body with earthy tones and fruity flavors, an intense purple color, and a vigorous, full-bodied taste. Malbec has turned into the best-known Argentinian wine, and it is considered a premium wine for export.

The weather and soil conditions are ideal for the growth of the malbec, especially in the Maipu River Valley of Mendoza. Malbec thrives in the "desert oasis" found in Mendoza in the slopes of the Andes. The malbec grape needs more sun and heat than other red wines.

Uruguay

After wine tasting in Mendoza, I next flew, by LAN Chile, to Uruguay to taste more wine and soak up some sun at the beach. My first stop in Uruguay was Montevideo. I selected the Hotel Ermitage, which is located in the cozy neighborhood of Pacitos. It had a good view of the ocean and included a breakfast buffet. This hotel had a good restaurant and bar and was popular with tourists because it was a good value.

Montevideo was first a Spanish fortress before eventually developing into a major port city. The Spanish first arrived in Uruguay in 1516. Montevideo was founded in the early eighteenth century. The natural harbor and proximity to the Rio de la Plata were favorable factors. The Spanish also introduced cattle, which became a major source of income. The city is noted for its architecture and styles.

Montevideo has four must-see attractions. The Plaza Independencia is a good starting point for sightseeing. It was originally a Spanish citadel, and it now marks the beginning of the old city. In the Plaza stands the statue of General José Gervasio Artigas, the father of Uruguay and leader of the independence movement. Many of the historic sites are adjacent to the Plaza and can be visited in a few hours.

Montevideo is known for its active nightlife—drinking, gambling, and dancing after midnight. Many of the popular bars are located in the coastal area of Carrasco and Pacitos. Check with your hotel desk.

A winery tour in Uruguay is a must. Uruguay does not have as many wineries as Mendoza, Argentina, but they emphasize small family wineries, which produce quality wines. My favorite winery was the Bodega Bouza, a boutique winery, the tour of which was arranged by my guide.

Bouza is a short drive from Montevideo. Bouza is a family winery, and they believe that working on a smaller scale produces better wines. Bouza produces a wide variety of whites, such as chardonnay. They also produce merlot and are noted for their tannat wines. The tannat wines have won Bouza many awards.

The tannat grape was imported mainly from the Bosque region of Spain. It has become the national red grape of Uruguay. Dense purple and red in color, tannat makes robust wines with aromas of smoke and plum. It has a long, generous finish.

Bouza also has a tour around the classic car museum, and there are walks one can take by the gardens and the organic vegetable garden.

After the wine making tour, we went to the gourmet Bouza restaurant, which served both lunch and dinner with the wine tasting. Wine tastings included four types of classic wines together with regional cheese. If you plan to go, it is best to make reservations. The hotel desk or your tour guide can make the arrangements. Tel. 598 2323 7491 or bouza@bodegabouza.com.

A must visit in Uruguay is Punta del Este, known as the Riviera of South America. Punta is a drive of about one and one half to two hours south of Montevideo on the South Atlantic. It is a narrow strip of land dividing the waters of the Rio de la Plata and the Atlantic Ocean.

Instead of a hotel, my travel guide booked me into a condominium that was fully equipped and had daily maid service. It was an excellent location at Punta del Este Triangulo (Avenida Francia and Yaro), with a beautiful panoramic view. To my right was the Rio de la Plata. To my left was the Atlantic Ocean. What a view! I could have stayed there forever.

In the summer season, Punta del Este was expensive. Nearby, on a side street of the condo, I found an inexpensive restaurant, the Asado, which was open nightly. It offered good food and service at a reasonable price. I dined there almost every night.

The Asado is decorated as an estancia and bar with tango music on the weekends. The wines are excellent. *Asado* means barbeque. Typically it is beef cooked on a grill, called a *parrilla*. Also, they have chorizos and chicken. Asado is a local favorite, usually accompanied by red wines and salads.

Punta del Este is a beach resort town on a peninsula. On one side, you have Mansa Beach on the Rio de la Plata. On the other side is Brava Beach on the Atlantic. Nearby is the famous Finger Beach where the giant hand with fingers emerges from the sand—a photo stop not to be missed.

My favorite beach is Brava, the one nearest to the condo I stayed in. This beach is directly across the avenue from the bus station. There is a restaurant on the beach and a beach bar, making it a good place to sit, relax, and watch the fun in the sun.

Because Punta del Este is on a peninsula, it is easy to explore by foot. The central street of Punta is Golero. This street is a popular shopping street with many sidewalk cafés for watching the passing parade of people. There is also a daily artists' market.

Punta del Este is famous for its nightclubs and bars. Most parties begin late and end around dawn. A popular night spot is the Conrad Resort and Casino. It has Las Vegas-style reviews and music. Shahira appeared there during my trip. There is music and dance and a twenty-four-hour casino. Another popular party bar is Moby Dick, at Rambla, near the yacht harbor. There is live music on the weekends.

I enjoyed my visit to Uruguay. It is a beautiful country with centuries-old Spanish traditions and warm, friendly people. Uruguay has some of the most breathtaking beaches in the world. And if you love sunsets, you will never want to leave.

The travel agent who helped me with my trip to Argentina and Uruguay is Diego Kraidelman, a native of

Uruguay. He grew up in Uruguay and knows the country as well as anyone. You will be in good hands with Diego. His company is:

Discover Uruguay
30 Woodland Street, Ste 11JK
Hartford, CT 06105
Fax: 1-800-247-6666
E-mail: ecouruguay@aol.com

12

El Camino de la Muerte, Bolivia: Buckle Your Seat Belt!

"A ship is safe in the harbor, but that's not
what ships are built for."
—Gael Attal

Most tourists begin their trips to Bolivia by landing in La Paz. The airport, El Alto, which is at thirteen thousand feet, is the highest in altitude in the world. Most visitors are not yet acclimated to the high altitude when they land. Some people need to take oxygen. Most of the hotels have oxygen available. Also there is coca tea. Coca is a leading crop and is used in tea to soothe and help acclimate the tourist.

The mountains of the Andes surround La Paz. A popular side trip for tourists is a drive into the Andes to travel the famous highway of death, known locally as El Camino de la Muerte. It also has the dubious distinction of being among the most dangerous highways in the world.

The road was constructed in the 1930s by Paraguayan prisoners captured during the Chaco War. Located thirty-five miles northeast of La Paz in the Yungar Region of Bolivia, this single-lane road is unpaved and has no guardrails, rendering it extremely dangerous. In the dry season, it is dusty with poor visibility; in the rainy season, it is muddy and wet. There are often mudslides and rockslides. The road is attractive to tourists because it is dangerous.

It is best to have an experienced driver and a sports utility vehicle (SUV) to travel this highway of death. Some two hundred people lose their lives each year on this road. Even buses have gone over the side of the road and tumbled down into the valley. It is even dangerous for bicycle riders. The side of the road is dotted with crosses marking the many spots where vehicles have fallen. Happily, a new, safer road is being built to bypass the old one.

Truckers use the road to haul cargo from village to village. Villagers use the buses that travel along this road as well. This road is the only connection between small Andean villages.

Which vehicle has the right of way when two vehicles, traveling in opposite directions, meet? The road rules specify that the downhill driver never has the right of way and must move to the outer edge of the road. Fast vehicles must stop so that passing can be negotiated safely. Sometimes the driver is forced to back up.

The local people have safety rituals when starting the trip; some pour a beer onto the dirt as a sacrifice to the ancient Incan earth goddess, Pachamama. This is a request that she hold onto you as you make your descent down the road.

Another popular side trip from La Paz is Lake Titicaca, the highest navigable lake in the world. It is ninety-four miles northwest of La Paz, near the border of Peru. The lake is known for its swaying reeds near the shores. The reeds are used to make boats, an ancient craft passed down to each generation.

A trip to Bolivia is an adventure, a step back in time. The landscape is beautiful, and the people are colorful. They hold onto their past grimly. Many wear colorful multi-layered dresses and lace. Women also wear English bowler hats.

13

Columbia SA. From the Mountains to the Sea.

"To Travel is to Live!"
—Hans Christian Anderson

My Latin America adventure took place in Columbia, SA starting in Bogota, only a five hour Delta flight from Atlanta, USA. The best way to describe Columbia is diversity. It is an intriguing country geographically traveling from Bogota to Cartagena. Landing in Bogota you are at 8,600 feet. Nice and cool weather in contrast to the hot Atlanta summer.

Descending the Andes, you travel through the coffee country at Pereira and to Cartagena at sea level on the Caribbean coast. The landscape is diverse and striking visually.

My first stop in Columbia was Bogota, a beautiful historic colonial city, the capital of Columbia. Locals refer to the city as the "refrigerator" because of its altitude in the Andes. There is a wealth of things to see and do for the visitor. Bogota is a city of museums, cafes, and fascinating Spanish colonial architecture. The visitor will never have a lack of things to experience.

My hotel in Bogota was the Hotel de la Opera, Bogota DC. Bario La Candetania, Calle de Coliseo, Calle 10 No. 5-72. Email sales@hotelopera.com.co. Fax. 571 537 4617. Single rooms range from 180 USD to 200 USD. The location is central and the hotel is clean and safe. This includes breakfast. There is a bar and small pool. It is located next to the Colon Theater and is a combination of two colonial houses. Across the street is the Palacio San Carlos, the government ministry of foreign affairs. The room has a balcony. There are two restaurants, La Scala and El Mirador. The bar is called El Automatico. On Fridays and Saturdays, there is live music entertainment.

The old colonial part of the Hotel Opera was once housed by Spanish settlers and later was used to house the personal guard of Simon Bolivar, the liberation hero with San Martin in South America. My hotel was booked by Gate 1/Discovery tours in the USA. Therefore, I got a group rate.

For the true budget travelers, there is the Hostel Sue Candelaria at 11.49 USD or North House Hostel at 11.00 USD in the Zona Rosa. A third choice is the La Nina Hostel, 21.00 USD, located Chapinero Alto, Calle 66 at 4-07, Bogota 571. La Nina includes a free breakfast. You can use HostelBookers.com.

Within easy walking distance of the Hotel Opera is Bolivar Plaza, or Square. Every Spanish colonial city has a central plaza with a large cathedral. This is a good place to start since it is the historical center. There is a monument to Simon Bolivar, the liberator, sculpted in 1846.

On the side of the Plaza is the Primary Cathedral of Bogota, built in 1823. The National Capital is located on the Plaza as well. It contains the Colombian Congress. The Palace of Justice can also be found in the Plaza. The plaza is fun for strolling around and watching the people. The Plaza is located between Calle 10 and Calle 11.

Next, I recommend visiting the museum del Oro, or Gold Museum. This museum has the largest pre-Hispanic gold collection in South America, more elaborate than Lima, Peru. It covers three floors of displays. The location is Calle 16 just off Carrera 7. Tel. 343-2222. www.banrep. gov.co/museo. Give yourself two hours to tour the gold museum. Be careful, you might get the El Dorado, or gold fever. There is a restaurant in the Gold Museum.

Next door to the Gold Museum is the Emerald Museum on the 23rd floor of the Arianca Building. This museum covers the subject of emerald mining and exhibits different size emeralds. It is all about emeralds. The collection is not as elaborate as the gold museum but well worth seeing. You will need an hour or less. The address is Calle 16 No. 6, 66 Edificio Avianca Building Piso 23, Bogota, Columbia in Candelaria. Tel 286 42 68.

The Botero Museum should be your next stop in Bogota. This museum exhibits paintings of Fernando Botero, perhaps the greatest painter from Columbia. Botero is famous for his paintings depicting large voluptuous women. Often his paintings include his image in the painting. Botero seems to reflect a sense of humor in his paintings. Botero was born in 1932 and is from Medellin.

Entrance is free to the Botero Museum. Besides his art work, you will see some works of Dali, Picasso, Monet, and other Europeans. The second floor is devoted to sculptures. There is a small shop and next door is the Casa de Moneda, or money museum.

Now, if you are ready to do some serious shopping for gold and emeralds, I recommend the Shop GMC, or the Galleria Minas de Columbia. Diagonal 20A No.

0-12. Bogota. Tel +57-12816523 + 57-1 3420552. Email ventras@galeriaminasdecolumbia.com. The shop is on the expensive side but they will bargain. Also, the quality is good and you get a certificate with each item. I only purchased a gold replica of an object in the Gold Museum. A good souvenir for my memories.

The next stop was to visit Monserrate Peak to visit the white church atop the peak. You reach the top of the peak by taking a funicular which is similar to a cable car but travels to the top by tracks. Also, if you have the stamina, you can hike to the top.

The panoramic view of the city from the top is impressive. Literally the city is laid out in front of you. The view is toward the West. The view is amazing.

Many people travel to Monserrate as a religious pilgrimage. The church was built in the 17th century with a shrine "El Senor Caido," or fallen Lord. The stations of the cross leads you on your walk to the church. There are also a restaurant, cafeteria, and souvenir shop.

The historical and cultural center of "Old Bogota" is La Candelaria. Many people start their tour from here. The visitor is attracted by the preserved colonial architecture. It is an excellent area for a walking tour. Restaurants can be found here too. There are small shops and colonial homes. During the academic year, University students can be seen. Many street artists.

Be sure to observe the basic security rules: i.e., beware of your surroundings, especially at night. It is safer in the day. Try to be in a group at night. You will see policia on almost every corner.

The next stop for my tour group was the large market "Plaza de Mercado de Paloque Mao." This is a traditional farmer's market and flower market. It is best to see this market in the mornings. The market has a variety of fruits and vegetables. The merchants will be happy to give you samples for tasting. The flowers are stunning in multi colors. A visual delight! The location of the Mercado is Cl 19 #26-04 Bogota.

Now a word about dining in Bogota. Historically the food is Creole but today it is fusion with the influence of Peru. Peppers and spices are used. Most often you will be offered "bistec" or beef accompanied by potatoes, corn, and rice with beans. Plantains are popular. There is chicken and on the coast, fresh seafood. Wine and "café", or coffee, are popular. The most popular beer is Club Columbia" cerveza, an amber lager. Founded in 1961 and it has won three international awards for taste. The other popular berbidos are Vino Tinto, or red wine, and rum drinks. The Cuba Libre is popular, rum and coca cola with lime. Chincha is a home —made beer made from corn and is popular with the locals. Also popular with the locals is Canelazo, a sugar cane drink. The Bogota Beer Company is a favorite for beer drinkers. Upscale bars are found in the Pink Zone, or Usaquen and T street. A more expensive area for bar hopping.

My tour group had a nice dinner with good service at La Bruja, Cl. 12 #3-45, La Candelaria, Bogota. Tel. 57 1 336 9261. The chef, who is from Peru, gave us a cooking class before the meal. Very informative and entertaining. The important part of the preparation was the mixture of spices, pepper, and creating a marinade.

The history of LaBruja has a fascinating story about a ghost and spirits. In 1916, the building was a seminary for priests and later a convent until 1948. In 1953 it was a prison for secret police. Executions occurred. In 1992, workers found a body in the walls. 2002, it became a restaurant and they discovered a ghost in the kitchen, Alvaro. Later Maria, another spirit was discovered. This is the origin of the name La Bruja. Many historic buildings in Candelaria are said to be haunted. The prices at the La Bruja are moderate. The atmosphere is excellent!

Next in the heart of La Candelaria is the restaurant El Gato Gris. Calle 13, Bogota. Tel 157 3421716. Barrio La Candelaria. Located in the historical district. Good service and the prices are reasonable. Most of our group had steak with red wine. Others had the fresh trout or chicken. Nothing fantastic. Nice setting. Good music. Its location brings in the customers.

El Gato Gris means grey cat. The story behind the name of the restaurant was a woman sat on the stairs and petted her grey cat. A passing man fell in love with her, so her husband moved them away. People never saw or heard from her again. The grey cat was lonely and roamed around the roof. Therefore the restaurant was named El Gato Gris, or the Grey Cat.

Before we departed Bogota, we made an afternoon trip to the Zipaquita Cathedral, or the famous Salt Cathedral just outside Bogota.

The new site of the Salt Cathedral was opened in 1995. This is the largest deposit of rock salt in the world. The mine extends 180 meters underground.

A main attraction of the tour inside is a depiction of the stations of the cross. There is a chapel and auditorium. It is often used for weddings. The temple at the bottom has three sections depicting the birth, life, and death of Jesus. Mass is held on a regular basis. Visitors have called it "Absolutely Amazing."

My group, Gate 1, next transported us to Pereira in the Coffee Zone. There we were lodged in the Hacienda San

Jose, a boutique hotel. Entrada #16, Valle del Cauca. Tel +57 6 3132612. This is a beautiful authentic Colonial hotel located in a beautiful setting of nature. You will never want to leave. The hacienda was built in 1884 and is decorated with colonial antique furniture.

I enjoyed after dinner sitting outside with my fellow travelers, having wine and swapping stories. During the day, there is horseback riding and bird watching. It is "paradise!" Unforgettable.

We arrive at the Coffee Plantation Recuca for our grand coffee adventure. We walk among the coffee bean plants, dress like workers, pick beans, and then gather to receive a lecture on the roasting process. Taste testing is also experienced. It is a complete lesson on the entire process. Very informative and educational. The coffee lover should not miss this trip.

A side trip to the botanical gardens is recommended. Butterflies galore in all their splendor in nature. Hummingbirds can also be seen.

Next we visit the Valle de Cocra, near Salento. Locals call this place "where the river begins." The valley is surrounded by beautiful green mountains which have popular trekking paths. Horseback riding is also popular. Europeans flock here for the hiking experiences. The views are spectacular.

Now we fly by Avianca to Cartegena on the Caribbean Seacoast. Its colonial history included its fortifications to prevent the invasion of pirates, or rival countries. Because it was here the gold and silver were put aboard the Spanish flotilla to be shipped to Spain. The city has a romantic charm. The colonial architecture is splendid! I spent days strolling the cobblestone streets in the old town and listening to the sounds of the salsa.

My hotel in Cartegena was the Urban Royal inside the walls of the old town. Located at centro cra.7 no. 34-10. Tel +575 645 5050. www.urbanroyalcartegena.com. You will want this hotel if location is paramount in your selection criteria. You just walk out the door and there you are. Everything except the beach. The average room rate is 150.00 USD. This includes breakfast. reserve@torredeloj.com.

Nearby is the interesting Museo de Oro, or Gold Museum at Centro Plaza de Bolivar/Bolivar Square, Cartagena. Tel 15 6600775.

The collection of pre-columbian gold is much smaller than the Gold Museum in Bogota. But worth a visit. It is organized well and easy to cover.

For shopping, especially Emeralds, I recommend the Casa de la Esmeralda in the center of the historic district near the hotel Urban Royal. Located at Centro, Historico Portal de los Dalces, Edificio Gonzalez Porto local 32-87. Tel 6609304. Email tilaesmeralda@yahoo.com.cartegena.

The casa offers a variety and sizes of emeralds at varying affordable price ranges. Each comes with a certificate. They are not opposed to bargaining. I bought a couple of rings and a necklace. They will do their best to match you with the right emerald for the best price for you.

As for shopping for the typical range of souvenirs, go to the tourist popular Las Bovedas. It is a strip of small shops which sell various typical cartegenian souvenirs. Las Bovedas are found in the old city and are attached to the fortress walls. They were built as dungeons. These dungeons now house shops. At one time they were used as prison cells.

If you are on a strict budget, you may decide to stay at the El Viajero Cartagena Hostel, just inside the historic wall city, located at Calle 7 Infantes, Cartagena. They offer dorms plus private rooms at 25 USD. Breakfast is included. There is air conditioning and use of the kitchen.

For nightly entertainment in the old city visit Donde Fidel Salsa Club located Centro, Plaza de los Coches, Old town, Cartagena near the clock tower and fountain. A beer and rum salsa club. Continuous salsa all night long. There is also an outdoor café.

Fidel was the favorite spot for Gabriel Marquez, the famous Nobel writer of Colombia. The salsa is non-stop. The rum flows freely. The beat of the salsa got to me and I tried the salsa on the dance floor. The crowd went wild and started chanting "El Papa." A night to remember. This is one of my favorite night clubs in the entire world.

My visit to the beach was La Boquilla near Cartagena. We traveled there to have a lunch of fresh fish. There is a line of palm thatched "enramadas" which prepare fish and seafood platters. The fish are the most fresh of Cartagena. We selected the thatched restaurant called "Marlane." Javier is the manager and service was excellent. Javier can also take you on a boat tour of the nearby mangrove to view birds and wildlife.

I took most of my meals at the Urban Royal Hotel restaurant Cafe del Reloj. The food is basic but not expensive. They have deli sandwiches, tortas, and postrez. Also pastas, crepes, and arroces. They do smoothies as well. Desayunos are available. Chilled fruit plates for the sun weary. Available are vinos, cervezas, and café or latte.

My final words about Columbia are all favorable. I enjoyed my tour of the country. Today it is safe. The cities are a mixture of the old and new. The countryside is lush and gorgeous. The culture is engaging. The people are friendly and eager to teach others about their country.

Reflecting on my tour of Colombia with Gate1, we started in Bogota, high in the Andes. This is a beautiful colonial city with much to offer such as the Museo Oro, the Botero Art Museum, and Colonial Candelaria. From Bogota we traveled to the coffee country or Zona Cafeteria. There we saw the beautiful Vallede Cocora, and visited a working coffee farm. The highlight for me was lodging in the Hacienda San Jose, a beautiful restored colonial home. Pure paradise. I hated to leave. But on we went. Next to Cartegena, a colonial city on the Caribbean. There we stayed inside the walled city and soaked in the colonial culture. We also enjoyed seafood by the sea. By night we moved by the salsa and rum. There was salsa music everywhere. What a trip! Who could ask for more? A trip to remember!

My trip was booked with:

Gate 1 Discovery Tours
455 Maryland Drive
Fort Washington PA 19034
800-682-3333
Gate1travel.com

I want to thank my guide, John David Comacho, and Samuel the Driver.

Muchas gracias amigos!

14

Nassau Bahamas. Argh Matey! From a pirates haven to colonial independence, Beaches, and Casinos.

"No man will be a sailor who has
contrivance enough to get himself into
jail; for being in a ship is being in a jail,
with the chance of being drowned."
—Dr. Samuel Johnson

Nassau is the capital of the British Commonwealth Nation of the Bahamas. It is located on the Island of New Providence, east of Miami and Cuba in the Greater Antilles. There are some 700 islands in the Bahamian chain. Nassau, in the early 1700s, was a haven or "nest" for marauding pirates. Today it is a magical mix of "Blackbeard and Blackjack." The Bahamas became an independent nation in July 1973.

The new treasure seekers can be found in the casinos, such as the world famous Atlantis on Paradise Island across the bridge from Nassau. The Wyndam on Cable Beach has the Crystal Palace Casino. The new BahaMar is planning an ultra large casino.

The beaches are world renowned for the white sand and crystal clear waters, especially Cabbage Beach on Paradise. Fishing, Scuba diving, or snorkeling will give you memories for a lifetime. There are dolphin encounters on the private Blue Lagoon Island. Shark and stingray adventures can be booked. Dive to see a shipwreck. There is something for everyone.

My hotel choice was the Wyndam Nassau Resort and Casino located on Cable Beach between the airport and Nassau. My room on the fifth floor had a balcony overlooking the ocean. The beach was superb. There was a large pool as well. I booked my room with hotels.com at 109.00 USD, no meals included. The Wyndam location is West Bay Street on Cable Beach, P.O. Box N-8306, Nassau 33312, New Providence Island, Bahamas. 800-207-4421. Casino Tel 327-6000. Hotel Tel. 327—6200.

According to the Nassau Guardian, the Wyndham will be demolished and re-developed along with the next door Sheraton. They will become a part of the Baha Mar group as a $3.5 Billion mega resort containing the biggest gaming floor in the Bahamas. The CEO did not give a definite timeframe for completion. The room prices should drop while this redevelopment continues.

Hotels are expensive in Nassau. The only budget hotel I could find is the Hotel Grand Central in Old Nassau just off Bay Street. Located on Charlotte Street, PO Box N4084, Nassau. Rooms are 69.00 USD. The rooms are cheap and a central location. It is cheap but you get what you pay for. It is perfect for the Nassau shopper and for seeing the annual Junkanoo. AC and cable TV. Internet in Lobby.

One of my favorite hotels in Nassau is the British Colonial Hilton. Rooms are priced at 129 USD. One Bay Street, Nassau. The only hotel in Nassau to have its own beach. Located at the western end of Bay Street. Great location for walking around, shopping, and viewing the cruise ships coming into the harbour. There are 288 rooms. Tel 322 3301 or www.hiltoncaribbean.com. Large pool facing the bay.

Probably the best Hotel is located on Paradise Island, the Atlantis. The Atlantis is a complex of hotels with a casino and water park. The Atlantis Royal Towers is 271 USD for a couple. It is a beautiful hotel, but has expensive food and drink. It is a massive resort. Service is excellent. The complex employs 6000 Bahamians. It is a great destination for a family because of the water park. Kids like it. Tel 363-3000 or www.atlantis.com.

Cabbage Beach on Paradise Island is near the Atlantis. Many find Cabbage Beach the most beautiful beach they have seen. The ocean water was warm, clear, and blue. In the high season it can become crowded since it is a public beach and the cruise ship people arrive. Also, there are many local people trying to sell you coconut drinks and souvenirs.

For quick food, I ate mostly across the street from the Wyndham and Sheraton at the Daiquiri Shack. The prices here for food and drink were much more reasonable than the large hotels. West Bay Street, Nassau. It can be reached by local mini bus No 10.

The Daiquiri Shack is a locally run business. The manager is often found on the premises and offers helpful travel advice. It is open to 11:30 pm. The Daiquiri Shack specializes in drinks blended from fresh fruit. My favorite was the mango with dark rum. The drink can be made as a "smoothie" without rum. The mango daiquiri is the best

I have ever had. Beer, water, and soft drinks are available along with snacks. They have tables outside. From the menu I made these notes:

Turkey or Club Sandwich .... $ 8.00
Hamburger with chips 6.00
Beer 3.00

Turkey was my favorite.

For more restaurant choices of a budget nature you can take minibus 10 into Nassau town. The bus will let you off on Bay Street, just beyond the British Colonial Hilton. You will find the various jewelry shops up and down Bay Street. Also, there is the straw market and the port for the cruise ships.

The Green Parrot Pub and Grill is located at #3 Prince George Wharf just off East Bay Street. Tel 323-7960. It is a perfect place to party or take a quick lunch while you are downtown. Draft beer is only $3.00. Sands beer is the most popular. They also specialize in Parrot Rum Punch.

From the menu, the Green Parrot offers:

Conch... $ 8.00
Salad 10.00
Wings 7.50
Burgers... 13.00
Turkey Club.. 12.00

The bartender is Eddie from the USA and has a wealth of knowledge about Nassau and the Bahamas. Ask him about the "swimming pigs."

For fast food and take-away for the real budget minded, try Jimmy's Take Away on Charlotte St. next to the Grand Hotel. The local favorite is"

Chicken, Rice, and peas .... $ 8.00
Conch... 9.70
BBQ 8.00
Turkey Sandwich.. 4.00
Sodas 1.00

Breakfast is also served.

An option for downtown dining is The Conch Fritters Bar and Grill directly across from the British Colonial between West St. and King St. on Bay Street. Tel. 356-9111

From the menu at Conch Fritters Restaurant I took these notes:

Grouper Burger.. $ 14.00
Conch Burger 14.00
Conch Fritters.. 10.00
Conch Salad... 12.00

I had the Grouper Burger. It was just satisfactory.

The traditional hamburger is $10.00 and a half rack of ribs is $17.00. Next door is a McDonalds on one side and a Dunkin Donuts on the other side of the Conch Fritter.

My personal favorite for eating like a local is to travel from Bay Street out to East Bay Street to the numerous restaurants underneath the Paradise Island Exit Bridge. This area is known as Potter's Cay. This is where the Bahamians came to buy seafood from the day's catch. You will see a long row of wooden fish stalls. You can walk around and visit the fishing boats and see the conch shells.

Conch and fish is king. Choose from Grouper or Red Snapper. Lobster is also available. Side orders are peas and rice, macaroni and cheese, fried plantains, cole slaw, and lettuce and tomatoes. For dessert there is Johnny Cake which is a Bahamian bread.

My favorite food stall is McKenzies. McKenzie is there every day chopping up conch to make salad and fritters. I had the Grouper and side dishes for $14.00 with a sand beer, a local popular beer. Beer is $3.00 A fish and conch combo is $15.00. Conch fritters are $3.00 and conch salad is $10.00. McKenzies food stall is the second one as you enter Potters Cay. Eat like the locals! Enjoy!

Next on my list is Twin Brothers food stall. It is a little more fancy with seating overlooking the harbor. The original is located at Arawak Cay. The area has developed into a number of restaurants and locally is called the "Fish Fry." It is on West Bay Street, a twenty minute walk from Nassau or just take minibus 10. The menus are similar.

Twin Brothers at Potter Cay offer seafood and daiquiris. It has been featured on NBC, CBS, and the NY times. From the menu here are my notes:

Snapper	$12.00
Grouper	12.00
Conch	10.00
Lobster	22.00
Conch Salad	12.00
Beer	3.50
Bahama Mama Rum Drink	12.00

While visiting Potters Cay, you may wish to walk down the dock to where the Bahama mail boats leave on a regular basis to visit the outer islands, such as Abaco. Abaco mail boat is named The Legacy.

Buying a ticket to travel on one of the mail boats is an economical way of visiting the out islands. Just walk up to the ticket window and purchase a ticket. The price on the Legacy to Abaco can cost 50 or 120 USD. It leaves at 7pm on Tuesdays and arrives on Wednesdays. You purchase a room on board the Legacy, or any similar mail boat. This allows you to visit Marsh Harbor and Turtle Key. Then you can stay over or return to Nassau on Friday morning. This is a cheaper way to visit the islands.

Ginger worked in the Legacy Office. The phone number is 601-5121. You get your ticket here at Potters Cay.

There are many options for activities in Nassau. My favorite is to visit Pirates of Nassau interactive museum depicting the role pirates played in the history of Nassau. It is located downtown at King and George streets. Just a block south of the cruise ship dock and the straw market. A must see for the history buff! Tel. 242 356 3759. www.piratesofnassau.com. Open 9am-6pm Monday-Saturday. 9am-12:30 pm Sunday.

Nassau became a virtual "pirates nest" in the early 1700s until Woodes Rogers became the Governor of the Bahamas and restored order 1718-1725. Roger was the first British Royal Governor of the Bahamas. Roger set up a gallows in Nassau and hanged the pirates to make his point.

The series of displays allows the visitor to see and experience the life of the pirate. You step onto the ship "Revenge." The sounds you hear are the sounds of the dock, the ship, and the local tavern. It is an interactive experience. The visitor enters the world of the "blood thirsty" pirates. You will come face to face with Edward Teach, the infamous "Blackbeard" himself.

As you walk through the exhibits there are trivia questions about the pirates. My favorite is: Did the pirates bury their treasures? The answer is no. They went into town and spent their money on rum and women!

Another favorite of mine to visit is the free tour of John Watlings distillery, a well-known maker of rum. It is a short walk up the hill from the British Colonial and Marborough Street. Walk up West Street. You will pass by the National Art Gallery. At Delancy Street turn right and there you are. 17 Delancy Street. (242) 322-2811. www.johnwatlings.com.

Watlings is located in the historic 1789 Buena Vista Estate. The tour is self-guided. It is also a store and tavern. Open seven days 9am to 5pm. In the tavern you sample several rums free.

Shopping is a favorite tourist reason to travel to Nassau because of the numerous duty free shops on Bay Street. Some people travel to Nassau for the sole purpose of shopping. You will find designer name watches, handbags, jewelry, and clothing. Some shops offer Bahamian arts and crafts, especially the infamous straw market. Some of the shops you will see are Colombian Emeralds, John Bull, Little Switzerland, Fendi, David Yurman, Gucci, Cartier, and Coach. Shop until you drop! Nassau is also a paradise for the shopper.

One of my favorite places to shop is the Coin of the Realm, located at Bay and Charlotte Streets. Tel. 242-322-4862. www.coinrealm.net. It was founded in 1977 by the Michael Stewart family, who are still the owners. The Coin of the Realm is housed in a famous gun powder magazine dating back to the 1700s. They sell coins dating back to the 4th century BC, Bahamian coins and gold. They also sell Sabo watches, Orbis jewelry, and pearls.

I collect historical coins. My most recent purchase was a coin salvaged from a Spanish shipwreck from the Coin of the Realm. A must stop is the Tortuga Rum Cakes and Rum. These make excellent gifts for the folks back home. The rum cake is moist and tasty. The medium size cake sells for 15.00 USD. Bicardi now has a rum cake store in Nasau. Tortuga Rum is located on Frederick St. near the wharf, also in the Lynden Pindling Airport.

On some of my trips to the Bahamas, I have chosen to travel to the Island of Bimini. Bimini is only fifty miles east of Miami on the other side of the Gulf Stream. Unlike Nassau, it is a laid back island, great fishing and diving. No traffic.

In the old days, I would travel from Miami to Bimini by the Chalk Air Sea plane, which has gone out of business. Now there is Tropic Air, which flies a seaplane from Miami and Ft. Lauderdale. www.flytropic.com 800-767-0897.

A new way to travel to Bimini is on the Super Fast ship from Miami. This ship has rooms, restaurant, and gambling. The fare is 49 USD round trip. www.ferryexpress.com 866-6988

Bimini was made famous by Ernest Hemingway who lived on Bimini in the 1930's. There he wrote "To Have and Have Not" while taking time to fish and drink. Locals tell the story that after one night of heavy drinking, he took a gun and walked down to the dock where he shot sharks in the water just for the sport of it. His experience in Bimini was his inspiration for "The Old Man and the Sea" and "Islands in the Stream." While in Bimini he stayed at the Compleat Angler Hotel and Bar which I got to visit. But it was destroyed by fire.

The U.S. Congressman from New York, the late Adam Clayton Powell, lived on Bimini. He had his daily ration of scotch and milk at the old End of the World Bar. The bartender, Bob, had numerous stories about serving Powell.

The famous Bimini landmark, The End of the World Sand Bar, was reconstructed in 2011. Like the old days, the floor is sand. This bar is North Bimini and Alice Town. It was "the" place to go. The owner hopes to recapture its lost glory. Enjoy a rum drink or Kalik beer. info@sandbar-bimini.com.

The Bimini Big Game Resort and Marina is a popular place to stay. It was founded in 1947 and located in Alice Town. Prices are from 179 USD. Tel. 800-246-8357.

For a place to eat, try the Anchorage Restaurant and Bar in Alice Town. Sample the conch fritters and conch salad. Sure to please, Joe's Conch Shack is another budget option. Hotel options in Alice Town are The Sea Crest Hotel or Big Johns Hotel. Now back to Nassau for the Junkanoo Festival.

A unique event to attend in Nassau is the annual Junkanoo parade and celebration. I attended one year. The event occurs December 26 to New Year's Day. This festival is similar to Mardi Gras in New Orleans and Carnaval in Rio. The climax and main parade is New Year's eve and New Year's day. It is an all-night colorful parade with music.

The parade marchers assemble on Shirley Street near Bay Street during the night. They march down to Bay Street and turn right to pass the viewers and judges. I was permitted to walk by the marchers preparing on Shirley Street. An unforgettable experience. Once the music starts, the beat will get you moving. It is a night to remember!

The various groups compete for first place and a prize. It is very competitive. My favorite Junkanoo group are "The Valley Boys." The other popular groups are the Saxons, One Family, and The Roots. The people eagerly await the judges' decision on New Year's Day. There is even a Junkaroo museum exhibiting the colorful costumes for posterity. For one night, Nassau turns into one big party. The James Bond movie, Thunderbolt, features the Junkanoo. It is one of the best outdoor parties you will ever attend.

The party is over and it is time to go home. There are many reasons to vacation in Nassau Bahamas. The Cable beach and Cabbage beach are two of the best in the world. Snorkeling, Diving, and fishing are top notch. The Bahamian cuisine is some of the best if you like seafood. Nassau is a short trip from Miami and the USA. There is no need for currency exchange. Bahamian people are friendly and hospitable. History buffs will find much to see and do.

Don't forget the world-class shopping on Bay Street. The night life and festivals are times to remember. In short, there is a wealth of activities. One will need to travel to the Bahamas more than once.

15

Karachi, Pakistan: July 4

"Home is where the heart is, and my heart is
wherever I am at the moment."
—Lily Leung

On my trip to Nepal, I flew Singapore Air and stopped
in Pakistan. My hotel was the Marriott Karachi. As
you know, Pakistan is an Islamic fundamentalist country.
Therefore, officially, there is no alcohol. I had lost track
of time, but I arrived there on the Fourth of July. Outside
the hotel, the taxi driver asked me if he could drive me
somewhere to have an alcoholic drink. I said, "Sure."

He took me to the nearby US Embassy, where the
ex-patriots were celebrating the Fourth.

At the embassy, I had to be interviewed at the gate and
show my passport. Then I had to have a sponsor to enter
the Fourth of July party. Soon, a tall Texan appeared to be
my sponsor. He was a petroleum engineer in Pakistan. He
had a distinctive Texan accent. He looked at my passport
and stated, "No American should be without a beer on the
Fourth of July." Then he invited me into the embassy. It was
one of the best Fourth of July parties I have attended. Plus
they had beer from the US—a perfect Fourth!

The Karachi Marriott Hotel is centrally located across from the Frere Hall and the park where cricket matches are played. The location of the Marriott made it easy to tour the city. The address of the Marriott is 9 Abdullah Haroon Road, Karachi, 10444 Pakistan. The phone is 92 21 3568011. Security at the hotel is excellent. Troops with machine guns guard the front door.

The National Museum of Pakistan is one of the most interesting museums to visit in Karachi. The museum exhibits historical relics that depict the development of Pakistan. Cultural relics are also on display. In the 1990s, a new section dedicated to the Quran was added.

Karachi can trace its history back to Alexander the Great. Alexander used the site in 326 BC as a seaport. The city is located in the south of Pakistan on the Arabian Sea. Today the seaport is important to the economic development of Karachi. In 1839, the British East India Company captured the city; the British annexed Karachi in 1843. Karachi was then linked to British India, and it continued to grow as a major Eastern exporting port.

Pakistan achieved independence in 1947. Many Muslim migrants from India settled in Pakistan. At one time, Karachi was the capital of Pakistan. Today, the capital is Islamabad. A must-see historic site in Karachi is the Jinnah Mausoleum, also called the National Mausoleum. Muhammad Ali Jinnah is the founder of Pakistan. Jinnah made his home in Pakistan in 1947. Actually Jinnah was born in Karachi.

The tomb is located in a central part of Karachi. Its size makes it highly visible throughout the city. I could see it clearly from my hotel room. It is constructed of white marble and sits on an elevated platform.

No trip to Karachi would be complete without shopping and bargaining in a Karachi market. My goal when I went to the market was to buy a carpet. I did not have to leave the Marriott because there were two carpet shops in the Marriott. One shop was called Afghan Carpet and the other Pak Carpets. They offered Pakistani, Afghan, and Persian carpets. Like I did, be sure to bargain if you go.

Another popular item to buy is a brass vase. Any metal ware with floral decorations makes a nice souvenir from Pakistan. The art of metal decoration was developed in Pakistan. There are many bazaars in Karachi selling varied merchandise. The Bohri Bazaar and the Urdu Bazaar are popular. The Zainab Market is within walking distance of the Marriott.

Karachi is also known as the City of Lights. In addition to what I've already mentioned above, there are many tourist sites that shouldn't be missed, including Clifton Beach. It is a trip well worth taking for the cultural experience and the historical edification.

16

Nepal: Hiking the Himalayas

"Take only memories; leave only footprints."
—Chief Seattle

I started my Himalayan adventure in Kathmandu, Nepal. My hotel was the Kathmandu Guest House, a famous hotel in Thamel, the center of Kathmandu's tourist district. It is convenient and affordable—ideal for budget travelers. There is a tour desk and restaurant.

My room upstairs on the back side had an excellent view of the Swayambhunath Stupa, or Monkey Temple, so named because holy monkeys live in parts of the temple. It is one of the most sacred Buddhist sites. It is famous for Buddha's eyes and eyebrows, which are painted on the stupa. You can easily reach it by taxi and tour on your own. It is an important site for Buddhists of several schools of thought. Even Hindus hold it in reverence.

After searching for a hiking guide, or sherpa, I secured the services of a guide and three porters for my hiking adventure. The guide supplied everything needed for the six-day hike—the tents, food, and the cookware. Basically, I did not have to supply anything nor carry anything. They walked with the supplies bundled on their heads. They had tremendous stamina and powerful legs.

We started our trek from Langtang, located north of Katmandu on the way to Tibet. After crossing the river, we immediately started walking up the hillside. At this level it is very green and pastoral. We reached a plateau and made camp for the night. The tents were set up. The view of the valley below was magnificent.

The next day we set out to cover more ground, always climbing higher. The trails were well established and were like a highway between the villages. We stopped from time to time to interact with the local people, who were friendly. It became a cultural experience.

We started in the tropical zone. The leaches were a problem. They attached themselves to our ankles to suck blood. We were constantly stopping to rid ourselves of the leaches.

Next, in a heavy rain, we came upon a village. The people asked us to stay there for the night. We gladly accepted. This was a good opportunity for a cultural experience. One home seemed to be the focal point. There we sat around the fire and conversed the best we could. One woman had a young child who was sick. The mother wanted to know if I had any medicine for her child. The child had a fever. I recommended an aspirin, but I cut the aspirin in half because a young child should never take an adult aspirin. The mother was happy with my efforts.

My tent was set up next to the goat pen. The next morning I was awakened by the goat farmer. He signaled to me that his goat had sick eyes. I agreed to look at the goat and treat it. The eye of the goat was inflamed, what we call pink eye. I treated the eye with an antibiotic gel. The farmer was happy.

Now it was time to depart the village and make our way back to Kathmandu. One of the young boys from the village followed our trekking group. He was going to run away from his family. He wanted to travel, but we insisted he turn back. He refused, but we kept insisting, and he finally turned back to home.

We eventually reached a high peak at about 12,000 feet. The Buddhist prayer flags flew in the wind of the stupa on the top of the mountain.

The Nepal trek was an amazing experience. I will remember the cultural experience forever. It is not considered a strenuous trek, but make sure you have a rain jacket and that you are in reasonable physical shape.

My sherpa's name was Tenzing, the same name of Sir Edmund Hillary's sherpa. I remain thankful to my sherpa and his porters for the experience—I say, "Namaste."

17

Easter Island, Chile: Were There Aliens?

"Man cannot discover new oceans unless he
has the courage to lose sight of the shore."
—André Gide

The best route to Easter Island from North America is by way of Santiago, Chile. This is the route I took. I flew LAN Chile to Easter Island. Easter Island is some two thousand miles west of Santiago, and the flight continued to Tahiti.

Chile annexed Easter Island, one of the most isolated islands in the world, in 1888. The culture of the island is part Polynesian and part Spanish. There are five thousand inhabitants today, and they are Chilean citizens. In Polynesian, it is called Rapa Nui. The nearest island is Pitcairn.

The Polynesians first discovered the island in about AD 400. Europeans found the island in 1772, when Dutch explorers landed there on Easter Sunday.

As a history major, I was always fascinated by the study of the huge stone statues on Easter Island. They are called *moai*. There are over eight hundred to be seen on the island. Traveling here to view them in person was a dream come true. Some are thirty feet high and can weigh twenty tons, although some weigh more. The largest statue is called Palo and weighs eighty-two tons. The statues are placed on stone platforms, called *ahu*. The most popular site of the moai is Ahu Akivi which has the only moai facing the ocean. The moai are spread out across the island; most are located near the coasts.

The moai have been the subjects of much curiosity and speculation throughout the years by tourists and academics. Why and how did the Rapa Nui people carve and transport these massive statues that surround the island? What happened to their culture? Some suggest that aliens may have played a role regarding these statues.

From what we know, the moai were religious symbols. The more statues you had, the more religious power you had as well. The statues were considered blessings. The moai were carved from volcanic rocks. In fact, you can travel to Rano Raraku, the crater where many of the Moai were carved. There are still scattered, unfinished moai which litter the hillside. It took hundreds of laborers, carving full time, to supply the statues that now exist.

How did islanders transport the moai from the quarry in the middle of the island to the coast? It is not certain, but speculation has it they used palm trees to roll the statues down to the coast. Of course, this contributed to deforestation. Also, the workers spent more time on the statues than on farming or fishing, which meant resources were depleted. The people grew restless, and violent disagreements began to break out. Their confidence in the old religion was lost. Many of the moai were toppled by the people.

The population was disappearing because of scarce food available. Some resorted to cannibalism. Also slave raids from Peruvians contributed to the demise of the culture and population.

Today the population has grown back to five thousand people. The major source of income is tourism. Of course the moai are the major attraction. The people are Chilean citizens and seem content.

The major village in Easter Island is Hanga Roa. Most of the tourist lodges are located there. There is a main street, and it is not uncommon to see someone on horseback. Riding horses is more economical than using cars or Jeeps. There are restaurants, pubs, and a market to buy souvenirs.

It is easy to fall under the spell of Easter Island, which is practically an open-air museum. A visit will fascinate and enrapture you. In fact, it is one of the most evocative places you will ever visit.

18

Papua New Guinea: In Search of the Bird of Paradise

"We wander for distinction, but we travel for
fulfillment."
—Hilaire Belloc

I arrived in Port Moresby, the capital of Papua New Guinea, on a flight from Australia. Papua New Guinea is an island and a nation. It was exciting to visit a culturally diverse and mostly unexplored country. I stayed in Port Moresby for two days. After visiting downtown, I visited the local yacht club. They allowed me inside after seeing my US passport. Inside I met several locals, and we drank beer together. The people were friendly and inviting. The next day, I visited the local golf club. Again the people welcomed me into their club.

When walking around Port Moresby, be careful to avoid stepping in the betel nut juice that the locals chew and spit out. The government has tried to enforce a no-spitting law, but chewing the betel nut is too popular. The betel nut acts as a stimulant and is used on social occasions. The drawback is that the red juice badly stains the lips and teeth.

After Port Moresby, I set off to the New Guinea highlands by small plane. I flew on a twin-engine, high-wing, Canadian De Havilland turbo. It was a missionary plane. The missionary-piloted planes are the best way into the interior because the roads are not well developed.

We followed the river, and our first stop was at a BP oil well. They had developed a gravel air strip. As we got closer to BP, we encountered some violent rainstorms. The pilot quickly went into a dive and got out of the rain clouds. When we landed, I was walking next to the pilot, who was an Englishman, so I asked him, "Why did we dive so suddenly?"

He answered, "I am so sorry, but when you find yourself in a rain cloud, the rule is to get out of it as quickly as possible."

After a short stay at the BP airfield, we boarded the plane to continue into the highlands. An interesting passenger boarded. He was an elderly man, native of Papua New Guinea, who wore only a loincloth and carried a bow in his hands. I had to show him how to be seated and fasten his seat belt. I knew I was in store for a step back in history.

We arrived in the southern highlands and were transferred to our jungle lodge near Mount Hagen. The lodge was on a hilltop with a clearing overlooking the jungle. There were numerous hiking and native trails.

We shared the lodge with a bird-watching group named the Victor Emmanuel Society. They were serious bird watchers with lots of equipment. Most people come here to view the Papua New Guinea (PNG) bird of paradise, which is not difficult to find. It is noted for its long, multi-colored tail feathers. The locals admire the bird of paradise, and during festivals, or *singsings*, they dress themselves up with colorful feathers.

We spent the days on hiking trips to view the nature around us and to view birds. Also, we visited villages to get to know the people and culture. In fact, I was invited to attend a colorful singsing and pig roast, which was one of the highlights of my trip.

The people had a history of cannibalism and head hunting before the missionaries arrived. The missionaries did their best to eradicate the philosophy of leverage in tribal warfare. Today the people of PNG are mostly agricultural, growing sweet potatoes and raising pigs. Locals are graded by how many pigs they own; that is how they determine wealth. Fishing is an important part of life in PNG as well.

According to the book by Macklin, the people of Asmat, New Guinea, practiced cannibalism into the early 1960s. In 1961, Michael Rockefeller, an anthropologist and son of Nelson Rockefeller, mysteriously and infamously disappeared while leading an expedition into the cannibal coast of New Guinea. The expedition's canoe was overturned by heavy seas, and they were set adrift. The speculation by the Macklin book is that Michael Rockefeller was eaten by either sharks or crocodiles. Rockefeller also could have drowned, or he might have swum ashore, where he was captured and sacrificed by the cannibals. It is jokingly said, "This was the most expensive meal the cannibals had ever eaten." Either way, the speculation about the fate of Rockefeller continues today.

I moved from the highlands to a beach area bordering the Bismarck Sea near Madang. There I stayed in a converted, palm-tree plantation house on the beach that had a swimming pool. The house had been converted into tourist rooms. Activities included sea kayaking and snorkeling.

During World War II, the Japanese had an airbase nearby, which can still be visited despite being somewhat overgrown. Bomb craters mark the landing field. I hired a driver of an aging Land Rover with a busted radiator to drive me to visit the Japanese airfield. It has only one Japanese "Betty" bomber remaining from an air raid by the allies. The plane is available to view for a small fee paid to the land owner.

Of course, the major air battle with the Japanese took place in Raboul, on the eastern Bismarck Sea. Japan planned to use PNG as a stepping stone to invade Australia. It never happened because of the fierce jungle fighting by the Allies; Australian and US soldiers stopped the Japanese in the famous battle of the Kokoda Trail in 1942.

I ended my journey to PNG by flying back to Port Moresby and on to Australia. It was a memorable journey, visiting new people and a unique culture on an island still in transition. Culturally and geographically, PNG is one of the world's least explored places.

19

Athens, Greece: Always Get a Receipt! It's All About History

"Travel teaches tolerance."
—Benjamin Disraeli

I arrived in Athens after visiting Cairo, Egypt. I did not have a hotel reservation, and it was during the busy vacation month of July. I had trouble finding a budget-class room, but eventually I found a room in a one-star hotel near the train station. The desk clerk negotiated with me on a room rate, and I paid him for the first night without getting a receipt—my mistake.

After staying there for about a week, I was told by a new hotel clerk that I had to pay my bill and leave for no apparent reason. He also said I owed him more money than I had negotiated with the first clerk. At first, I wanted to go to the police, but I decided to pay his price because he said the first clerk had died and I owed the bill. So I gave in, paid the inflated rate, and checked out. Clearly, I had been taken, but I still paid. The lesson for me was that I should always get a receipt.

I found another hotel, which I highly recommend, owned by honest people—the Hotel Carolina, 55 Kolokotroni Street, Athens 10560, Greece. The Carolina has been renovated and is now a two-star superior hotel. There are thirty-one rooms with balconies. The rooms are comfortable and clean with modern facilities. There is a complimentary breakfast. The rates are about eighty US dollars. I first stayed there in 1991, and the staff was friendly and helpful. Today it has new ownership.

It is impressive because of the historical building in which it is located. It has a great location near the Plaka, or old town, near the Acropolis and the Parthenon. The metro station is nearby, as are numerous cafés.

An excellent restaurant choice near the Plaka is the Platanos. It has been at its location since 1932. There are tables on the square in the front. The Platanos is known for its Greek cuisine and wines. The menu is appealing to the budget traveler.

The most popular tourist attractions are the Acropolis and, atop the Acropolis, the Parthenon. This fortress dates as far back as the thirteenth century BC. The Parthenon is a model for Western architecture.

My favorite museum in Athens is the Archaeological Museum, located at 44 Patission Street. This museum houses a huge collection of Greek artifacts. Also there are sculptures, such as renderings of Zeus and Apollo, and hand-painted vases.

Another favorite of mine in Athens is the National Historical Museum, 13 Stadiou Street, near Omonia Square. The museum is a catalog of Greek history ranging from the Byzantine era up to the War of Independence.

My favorite excursion outside Athens is to Delphi. I took a full-day bus tour by American Express. It was a scenic drive through the farmland and up into the mountains. Of special interest was an early Olympic stadium and the site of the Delphi Oracle. Be sure to look at the old graffiti on the stadium.

The budget traveler will find the city of Athens is a great value, especially considering the present day economic turmoil. The historical sites and museums are a dream come true for the history addict, and the Parthenon is awesome. This is a trip to remember.

20

Kathmandu, Nepal: How to Buy a Buddha

"Experience, travel—these are an
education in themselves."
—Euripides

I have always been intrigued by Buddhas. They represent
serenity and peace. Before leaving Kathmandu, I set out
to shop for a Buddha. I walked down Thamel Street, going
from shop to shop, comparing Buddhas and prices. Finally,
at one shop late at night, I found the Buddha I wanted.
The shop owner appeared to be from India. We bargained
for the price, and we eventually agreed and closed the deal.

The Buddha I selected is called an enlightenment
Buddha. It is bronze. The right hand is facing downward
with fingers extended toward the ground and the palm
facing inward. It is seated with ankles tucked. This Buddha
represents insight, purity of character, and self-mastery.

I admire my Buddha constantly at home. The Buddha
reminds you of what you are trying to attain: the middle
way or self-perfection. Man is supposed to follow the four
noble truths and the eightfold path—the right conduct.

Buddha lived around 500 BC in Northern India. His
philosophies became the foundation of Buddhism. Buddha

statues show him with various hand gestures, called *mudtas*. To find the right Buddha for you, choose the statue that makes you feel the best.

My hotel was the Kathmandu Guest House in Thamel. For shops, bars, and restaurants, simply walk out the front gate and turn left. Immediately you will encounter many small and privately owned shops. They sell a variety of goods, ranging from trekking clothes, hats, bags, and statues of Buddha. Everyone is willing to bargain, so don't be shy to ask for the best price. Offer half the price you are quoted. Shopping in Thamel is fun! Thamel is mostly shops.

The Pilgrims Book House is a popular gathering place. It has a nice eating place in the back of the shop. Try K2 restaurant for a good steak.

A rickshaw is a fun and exciting way to travel around Thamel. They are not expensive. It is a once-in-a-lifetime experience.

Every day, at home, I admire my Buddha. It gives me much pleasure and reminds me of the spiritual potential within all of us. It is serene. Shopping for a Buddha statue is an adventure in Kathmandu. I mean no disrespect for my purchase. It was fun to visit various shops and to compare and bargain. Namaste!

21

Istanbul, Turkey: Mosques, Ancient Troy, and the Grand Bazaar,

"The world is a book, and those who do not
travel read only a page."
—St. Augustine

There is no other city like it. Istanbul, located on the Bosporus Strait, is where West meets East. European culture and Asian culture meet and create an atmosphere not to be found anywhere else. You can experience exceptional architecture and history there. Shop the Grand Bazaar, visit mosques and Byzantine churches. Enjoy small cafés. Visit glamorous nightclubs. Enjoy incredible food and coffee. Get ready to bargain. Istanbul is one of the world's great cities. It is a multi-cultural experience. The bazaar awaits you.

I began my tour of Turkey in Istanbul. My hotel was the Aziyade Hotel. The architecture was in the Ottoman style, and it was in the Sultanahmet district, or the old city, of Istanbul. From the hotel, it was a ten-minute walk to the Blue Mosque. The Grand Bazaar was about half a mile from the hotel. The location was excellent. The hotel had a great staff and service. At the top of the hotel was the Panorama

Restaurant and Bar with a great view of the Marmara Sea. It was modestly priced at forty-three US dollars per night, a good value for the money. Also, it was near the tram.

The address is Piyerloti No. 30, Cemberitas, Beyazit 34490 Istanbul. aziyadehotel.com. I booked my hotel and tour with Pacha Tours NYC. Tel. 1-800-722-4288. They offer escorted tours and tailor-made travel.

Historically, Istanbul was the capital of the Roman Empire. Later it became the capital of the Byzantine Empire. The name changed to Constantinople. Then, in 1453, Istanbul became the final capital of the Ottoman Empire. Istanbul has taken its place in world history. It is no longer called "the sick man of Europe."

The most popular tourist attraction in Istanbul is the Blue Mosque, which has six minarets. It is called the Blue Mosque because of the blue tiles used in the construction of its floors. It was constructed circa 1616 by Sultan Ahmet Camii. The central prayer area is huge.

Other sites to see are the Hagia Sophia, which was built during the reign of Byzantine Emperor Justinian and completed in AD 537. It was first a church and then a mosque. It is Istanbul's most famous monument.

Of course, no visit is complete without a visit to the Grand Bazaar. It is located in the heart of the old city. The bazaar is a maze of some two thousand shops. It is an opportunity to try your hand at bargaining, which is a way of life here. You can find all types of goods here. Carpets, silver and copper works, lanterns, leather, jewelry, etc.— one could spend days here.

I personally found the bargaining difficult in the bazaar. The shop owners have become jaded after so many years. I found better bargains in the shops just outside the gates. But give it a try. It is a shopper's delight.

Another historic site to visit is the Topkopi Palace. Work started on the palace in 1453, and it became the home of the Ottoman Sultans. The palace is a showcase of the treasures of the old city.

Next I traveled outside Istanbul to visit the great city of ancient Troy. I traveled across the Bosporus and into the North Aegean coast of Turkey. This area was occupied by the Greeks. Homer's *Iliad* made Troy famous. Troy was founded during the Bronze Age (3000 to 1700 BC). Historians conclude that it was Troy VI or Troy VII who was involved in the legendary Trojan War. Later Constantine the Great considered making Troy the capital of the Eastern Roman Empire. The name "Troy" became synonymous with the word "war."

Paris was the son of the King of Troy. Paris eloped with Helen, Queen of Sparta. This was the cause of the Trojan War, according to Greek legend.

At the entrance to the ruins of Troy stands a replica of the wooden Trojan horse. One can climb up inside the horse and have a panoramic view of Troy and its outer walls. As I viewed Troy, I could visualize Homer's epic tale of the Trojan War, which immortalized Helen, Paris, Agamemnon, Achilles, and Hector.

Next I visited Ephesus, the birthplace of the Virgin Mary. One can still visit the house today. This is one of the best places in Turkey to visualize an ancient Roman city. Here one can visit the ruins of the Temple of Artemis, rebuilt by the Greeks in 550 BC. Artemis is considered to be one of the Seven Wonders of the Ancient World and a must-see for every tourist or history buff when traveling to Turkey.

An essential to visit in Turkey is Cappadocia. It is an earthen museum composed of cave dwellings—a city composed of caves. There are even rock-cut churches with frescoes. You might choose to stay in a cave hotel. Cappadocia is also noted for its early morning hot-air-balloon tours.

Turkey offers an amazing vacation destination. I am one who enjoys history, culture, and architecture, which is why I found Istanbul diverse and exciting. I also enjoyed Troy and Ephesus. My interaction with the local people was enjoyable and educational. One can only benefit from such an educational tour. Turkey is indeed a richly historical country.

22

Amsterdam: Rembrandts, Beer, and Walking the Streets

"Travel is not the time to break in new shoes."
—Lynne Christen

Amsterdam is one of my favorite cities. The people are friendly and enthusiastic. They enjoy life in Amsterdam. The nightlife is active. I especially enjoy the numerous cafés, bars, and sidewalk cafés for sitting and watching the passing parade of people. The restaurants serve food from all over the world.

Amsterdam is also noted for its numerous museums—especially the Rijksmuseum for the Rembrandts and the Van Gogh Museum. Amsterdam contains some forty-two museums. It is indeed "museum land."

I visited Amsterdam on my own, not on a group tour. It is a compact city, and as a pedestrian or a cyclist, it is easy to move around. There are more bicycles than autos. It is estimated there are over twelve million bicycles in the Netherlands.

For my hotel, I selected the Hotel Prinsenhof. It is a budget-class hotel in a renovated canal house near the area of Leiensplein on the Prinsengracht Canal. A single room without bath is about sixty US dollars and includes a Dutch breakfast. A hand pulley will lift your luggage from the street.

If you prefer a more modern hotel, try the Park Hotel or the Marriott nearby in Leidensplein, but you'll forfeit the historical setting of the canal house. I have also stayed in the Hotel Wrechmann at 288 Prinsengracht. It, too, is a canal house hotel, but most rooms come with private baths. It is not far from the house of Anne Frank. It includes a large Dutch breakfast.

My favorite museum to visit is the Rijksmuseum. There you can view the Rembrandts and the seventeenth century collection of Dutch masters. Rembrandt's *The Night Watch* is a must see. It was painted in 1642. In the surrounding rooms you will see the paintings of the Dutch masters. Rembrandt represents the Dutch Golden Age in paintings. The museum's collection consists of almost one million objects. This includes Delftware, which Holland is noted for.

The Rijksmuseum can be easily reached by tram, canal bus, or on foot from Leidseplein. Just go east a short distance from Leidseplein square. This museum ranks up there with the British Museum in London. The exact address of the Rijksmuseum is Jan Luikenstrast 1, just off the canal.

Directly in back of the Rijksmuseum is the Van Gogh Museum. The most famous paintings of Van Gogh, such as *The Potato Eaters* and *Sunflowers*, are located here. Other museums are the Maritime Museum, the House of Anne Frank, the Amsterdam Historical Museum, and the Rembrandt House.

The Heineken Brewery Museum and tour are popular. The museum is a short walk from the Rijksmuseum, and daily tours are provided so one can learn how the beer is brewed. Even though it is no longer a working brewery, the tour ends with a beer tasting of this very popular beer, which was first established in 1814.

Walking tours and bicycle tours are popular. You can take a bicycle tour outside the city and view the waterways and windmills. A canal boat tour is recommended. There are boats you can embark and disembark, just like buses. It is the best way to view the old canal houses. You will also get a feel for the maritime history of the city. Bars and café sitting are popular in Amsterdam. This is my favorite activity.

Leidseplein and Rembrandtsplien are good locations for bars and cafés. In Leidsplein I enjoyed going to the Bulldog Bar and Café. The activity seemed to always be lively there. The crowd was mostly young, but everyone fit in. The music was loud and non-stop. The Heineken flowed freely. Also, the Dutch drink, *ginever*, or Dutch gin, was a popular choice. Cannabis sales are available here although there is a movement from the city government to regulate cannabis sales. The older, original Bulldog café, which the owner named after his pet dog, is still open just outside the sailors' quarters, near the red-light district.

Outside the front door of the new Bulldog is the twenty-four-hour Sports Bar & Café. Sports from all over the world are constantly on the TVs. They are also known for their full English breakfast. There is an outside café, and they serve pancakes.

Next door, near the tram tracks, is the Café Heinekin Hoerk, or corner bar and café. In the summer it has an excellent sidewalk bar and café. The menu has a variety and is very reasonable. This is quiet compared to the Bulldog.

For those who prefer a taste of home, there is a Burger King and McDonald's in Leidseplein.

I admire Amsterdamers' enthusiasm for life. Whether you spend three days or a week, the days and nights will pass quickly. Enjoy the philosophy of Amsterdam: "Live and let live." You will more than likely make a return visit.

23

Churchill, Canada: The Polar Bears

"Without new experiences, something inside
of us sleeps. The sleeper must awaken
—Frank Herbert

I have always wanted to see polar bears up close and in their natural habitats instead of in a zoo. I decided to take a polar bear tundra buggy tour out of Churchill, Manitoba, Canada, to observe and photograph the annual fall migration of the polar bears.

For this tour I selected Travel Wild Tours. There were many options, but I selected Travel Wild because it was reasonably priced and the quality of the tour was very good. There are Natural Habitat Adventures and Tundra Buggy tours as well. A group tour is the best way to see the polar bears.

I flew on the now defunct Northwest Airlines from Atlanta to Manitoba. I spent the night in the airport hotel, from which I was able to visit the city on the way in and, later, on the way out. It was enjoyable to meet our Canadian friends to the North. I enjoyed touring Winnipeg and shopping for winter clothing at the Army Surplus. The pubs were good also. I was introduced to Labatt's Blue Beer, the local favorite. All I needed to say was "I want a Blue."

We flew a Calmair Convair prop plane north to Churchill. It was some 1,100 miles to Churchill from Winnipeg. The aircraft was basic and also delivered cargo. The airport runway was built by the US as part of the Cold War defense system. We were also given the choice to travel by rail to the northern terminus of the Hudson Bay Railway. The train is used to ship grain south in season.

Churchill, Manitoba is called the polar bear capital of the world. Churchill is a small town on the shore of Hudson Bay. Every fall, hundreds of polar bears pass through Churchill in their annual migration. They come out of summer hibernation and go toward Hudson Bay to wait for the pack ice to form. When it forms, they can roam and hunt for seals. They can eat seal blubber and fill up. They are hungry bears.

We used Churchill as our base camp because it features several small hotels. Ecotourism is the mainstay of the town's economy. During my trip, we spent each night in a small hotel in Churchill. Each day we took a tundra buggy to view the landscape and photograph the polar bears. Today the tourists stay in tundra-buggy hotels instead of land-based hotels. By staying in town, we could walk around and mingle with the local people. This included the Inuits, who carve magnificent souvenirs from stone. There was also the Eskimo Museum, where we could buy souvenirs.

Churchill is unique in that it has a polar bear jail. If polar bears wander into town—usually in search of food or garbage—they are captured and held in stalls in one of the old hangars at the airport. In a way, they are taught behavior modification by taking away their freedom. After a time they are marked with paint and air lifted out of town in a net below a helicopter. They are taken north and released.

Tourists usually travel by tundra buggies, modified school buses fitted with large tires to make it impossible for the bears to reach up into the cabin. There was a heater on board, and I found our buggy to be safe, warm, and comfortable vehicles. The elevated cabin was excellent for viewing and photographing the bears. There was a guide on board to explain what we were seeing and explaining the behavior of the bears.

Ecotourism is the mainstay of the economy of Churchill. The town has a school, a hospital, several hotels, restaurants, bars, a rail line, an airport, and a port with a grain elevator. Many guides claim the annual migration seems to be getting later every year, perhaps because of climate change. You'll see the most polar bears in Churchill in October and November.

Polar bears are classified as an endangered species. The bears are found mainly within the Arctic Circle. It is the largest carnivore in the world. Only the Kodiak Bear rivals it in size. Biologists estimate there are about twenty thousand to twenty-five thousand polar bears worldwide.

Primarily, the polar bear hunts seals, which are abundant in the Arctic. The bear uses its extraordinary sense of smell to hunt. First, it finds a hole in the ice and waits there for the seal to surface for air. Then, the bear reaches into the water and drags the seal out onto the ice. Another method of hunting is to stalk the seal resting on the ice. Some polar bears have been known to attack the walrus. They have also preyed upon beluga whales.

My hotel in Churchill was the Tundra Inn B&B, located near the center of town at 34 Franklin Street. The rooms were well maintained, reasonably sized, and had a fridge. There was a pub and restaurant. Travel Wild booked the room for me.

Another popular hotel is the Lazy Bear Lodge. It is a unique handcrafted log hotel. The Lazy Bear is located at Kelsey Boulevard and Button Street. The Lazy Bear Café adjoins the hotel and also has the log-cabin setting. The menu offers a variety. You can choose caribou steak, Arctic char fish, Hudson Bay trout, or fillet of cod.

Gipsey's Bakery is another popular eatery. It is known as a local hangout. They use a walk-up counter for service.

Churchill is the only place on earth where the tourist can see the annual gathering of polar bears in such large numbers. There is amazingly close viewing and photography of the polar bears. It is exciting to see the young bears play. Churchill is nature's delight, an unforgettable experience.

24

Berlin, Germany: No Longer Two Germanys

"Not all those who wander are lost."
—J. R. R. Tolkien

B erlin is one of my favorite cities. It is a special place for me because I visited there just after the wall came down in 1989. The Soviets had divided Berlin into East Berlin and West Berlin. The Soviets built the wall in 1961 to stop the flow of people from East to West. The educated people of the East were flowing to the West, where the opportunities were better. Presidents Kennedy and Reagan asked the Soviets to tear down the wall. It was a remarkable time in history.

My hotel was in the old West Berlin. I selected the Hotel Bogota. This is a budget hotel and a good value at about sixty US dollars for a single. This includes breakfast. Not all rooms have a private bath and toilet. The hotel is housed in a century-old building. The hotel is a short walk to the famous street of Kufurstendamm, or as the locals call it, Ku'damm, which is several miles long and starts at the Kaiser-Wilheim Church. Nearby is Bahnhof Station, Berlin's main train station.

Ku'damm is noted for its many shops. On this street you will find the famous Kadewe department store. It is not only for shopping but also for food and restaurants. I ate there frequently. The other well-known street is Unter den Linden. It is on the other side of the zoo and parallels the Tiergarten. Unter der Linden is the main east-west boulevard through Berlin. The boulevard extends from above Humbolt University in the east and to the west past Tiergarden. It got its name from the rows of Linden trees planted there. Duke Friedrich Wilheim planted the trees in the mid-1100s.

Start your walk at the zoo and then go toward old East Berlin. At the top end is the famous Brandenburg Gate. To each side of the gate stood the wall that separated Berlin. As you walk up Unter den Linden, you will see the Victory Column. It is a victory statue of the golden goddess of victory, which stands upon a granite column. You can climb up to the top if you are in shape. It offers a great view. It is one of my favorite tourist sites.

Next you come to the Brandenburg Gate. It is a very important tourist attraction because it was formerly the dividing point of East and West Berlin. Atop the gate, there is a chariot drawn by four horses and driven by Victoria, the Roman goddess of victory.

One block north of the gate is the Reichstag building. The Reichstag was the Parliament of the German Empire. It opened in 1894. Later, as events occurred, it fell into disuse until it was restored after reunification of Germany in 1990. Now it is the meeting place of the modern German parliament, the Bundenstag.

As you continue walking down Under den Linden from the gate, you come across the Humbolt University of Berlin. It is Berlin's oldest university, having been founded in 1810. After reunification, the university was restored in the western model of education. Today it has some 27,000 students.

The university is open to visitors and tourists. I stopped in and had lunch in the student cafeteria. The lunch was affordable. The lunch with drink was less than five dollars. Also I got to mingle and converse with the students and visit the bookstore.

Just outside the university, on historic Under den Linden, is the statue of Fredrick the Great, a massive bronze statue built about 1839. Fredrick is atop his favorite horse. It is worth viewing.

From here you can walk to Museum Island in old East Berlin. This area is known for the Pergamon Museum that houses artifacts from ancient Greece as well as middle-eastern art and architecture. It is named for the Pergamon Altar, an art possession from Greece. It also contains the Gate of Ishtar.

Continue walking eastward and you will come upon Alexander Platz, which is essentially the heart of old East Berlin. There is a large pedestrian plaza, making this an ideal café sitting area to observe the passing parade of people. Of interest nearby is the impressively tall TV tower. It houses an observation desk for excellent views of Berlin when it is not foggy. The observation deck also has a bar and restaurant.

Checkpoint Charlie is a must-see in East Berlin. During the Cold War, it was the only border crossing between East and West Berlin that permitted passage to foreigners. This has been the subject of countless spy novels and movies. There was a guardhouse and the infamous "You are leaving the American sector" sign.

Nearby, in a small museum, exhibits from Checkpoint Charlie and devices used by East Berliners to escape to freedom in the West are on display. It is located at Friedrichstrasse 44.

Most of the Berlin Wall has been torn down. For posterity and the tourists, there is a remaining section of the wall. A large section can be found to the east of the city center along the River Spree in Muhlenstrabe.

To the right of Brandenburg Gate was the area of Hitler's underground compound where he died as Berlin fell at the end of World War II. There is no memorial there. Berliners have rebuilt and repaired the buildings in old East Berlin, which has been rejuvenated.

The best places to eat or snack if you are on a budget are the large number of food stalls called Imbiss. Essentially, this is street food found all over the city. Here you can buy wurst, hot dogs, French fries, cola, and beer at reasonable prices. Plus the food is usually good.

My favorite place to shop and bargain in Berlin is in the flea market. My favorite flea market is located at the lower end of Unter den Linden, near the zoo and Tiergarten. There you can find numerous antiques and curios. You never know what you might find. It is fun to look and bargain.

Berlin is a huge city. There is much to see and do. You have to pick and choose and maybe have more than one visit like me. I have traveled to Berlin three times.

25

Munich Bavaria. A city and state of many travel choices.

"We live in a wonderful world that is full of
beauty, charm, and adventure. There is no end
to the adventures we can have if only we seek
them with our eyes open."
—Jawaharial Nehru

Munich, founded 850 years ago, is the capital of
Bavaria and the gateway to sightseeing in Bavaria.
Munich means "the home of Monks." Because it was
founded by the "Munichen" monks. There is an abundance
of things to see and do in Munich and the surrounding area
of Bavaria. It is your choice. You will need to be organized
and selective depending upon your available time. Munich
is a great city for the history buff. There are many museums.
The architecture is splendid. In Bavaria there are an
abundance of castles.

My hotel choice was the Litty's Hotel located centrally
only two blocks from the train station. The Litty Hotel
is located at Landweh Str 32c, Ludwigsvorstadt 80336
Munich. Phone +49 89 54344211. Fax +49 89 54344212.

www.littyhotel.de or info@littyshotel.de. A single room with bath share can range from 52 USD to 62 USD. This includes a generous breakfast. A night clerk is on duty the entire night. There is no curfew.

Value and location is excellent! The Litty is only a five minute walk from the Munich Central Train Station and a ten minute walk from the Old Town or Marienplatz. The room was clean and safe. A sink is in the room and the room has nice hardwood floors. Also, there is a TV and elevator. It is a good value for your money. Every three rooms share the shower and toilet. I enjoyed my stay at the Litty!

Another hotel choice located not far from the Hauptbahnhof, or train station, is City Hotel with bar and restaurant. Located at Schiller Strasse 3q. 80336 Munich. Tel +49 (0) 89-4613 53-225. www.city-aparthotel.de

City Hotel is a traditional hotel by USA standards. The rooms are large and very clean. Rooms include A/C, TV, and WiFi. Includes toilet and bath. Great location near train station. Includes breakfast buffet. Price is moderate at 106 E. for a single. The address is Schillerstrasse 3a, Ludwigsvorstadt, 80336, Munich Tel +49 (0) 89-46 1353-225

Hotel Atlanta is another good choice at a moderate price. Atlanta is located at Sendingserstr 58, Altstadt Lehel, 80331, Munich, not far from Karlsplatz. A single with shared bath is 54 E, and a single with bath is 74 E. The location is perfect for sightseeing and Octoberfest. Rooms are clean. Tel +49 (0) 89-46 1353-225. There are three flights of stairs. Breakfast is good.

The Hotel Metropol has full room accomodations and is worth the extra money for those who want a room above the budget class. The Metropol is near the train station and has been recently remodeled into a modern hotel. The rooms are big and spacious. The Metropol is located at Mittererstrassee 7, 80336 Munich. Tel 1-888-614-1750 or 011 49 89 24449990. A superior single is 145.00 E and a superior double is 170.00 E. It is worth the extra Euros.

Wombat's Hostel offers the cheapest budget class rooms. Hostel world calls it the "World's Cleanest Hostel." The rooms offer A/C. There is an attractive glass roofed courtyard, nice for relaxing in winter or summer. Wombat's has become a budget class institution in Munich. There is no age limit and no curfew. The location is near the train station and old town. The address is Senefelderstrasse, 1 80336 Munich. Phone is +49 89 59989180. Room rates at Wombat's are 38.00E for a private single and the dorm can range from 15.00 to 18.00 E. A locker is supplied. Breakfast is extra. There is a popular bar. You can meet fellow travelers from all over the world and share travel stories. Wombat's is everything you want in a hostel.

Munich offers almost endless choices for dining especially if you like pork and sausage prepared in the Bavarian style. Most dining places are found in the city center, especially around the train station and Marienplatz. Beer is an important part of the meal. Beer is called "liquid bread." Munich has six breweries and is the host to the famous Octoberfest. It is an annual event occurring from mid-September into early October. A sixteen day beerfest!

My favorite outdoor café is the Bohne and Malz Restaurant and Bar in Marianplatz. They also have indoor dining if the weather turns foul. Outdoor cafes are popular. This popular café is directly across from the famous Rathaus, or New Town Hall. The Glockenspiel is located in the Rathaus facing the Café. It is a mechanical clock which depicts a German jouster on horseback fighting a French jouster. A Bavarian dance follows on the clock. The crowd loves it. An ideal place to sit and see the changing of the Glockenspiel at 11am or 5pm. The Rathaus is an ornate building and dates back to the 12th Century. This is a focal point for most tourists. A must see. Munich was heavily bombed in WWII. Most buildings were restored using the original architectural plans.

Some ideas from the menu at the Bohne and Malz are:

Weiner Schnitzel .... 17.80 E
Soup 4.80
Chicken Breast 13.00
Grilled Salmon 15.00
Greek Salad 11.80
Baked potato filled with mushrooms
    & herb Cream with salad 8.90
Beer 4.50
Merlot 4.80
www.bohneundmalz.de.

Another outdoor café is the Schnitzelwirt Im Spatenhof. It is in front of Suturn Electronics and across from Louis Vitton. It is adjacent to Karlsplatz on upper Neuhauser Str. Before reaching Marienplatz. No. 39 Neuhauser Str, 80331 Munich. Tel 089 264010. They also have an indoor café. www.schnitzelwirt.de.

No trip to Munich is complete until you visit the Hofbrauhaus, Platzl 9. It is the oldest and most famous beer hall in the world. It is located in the center of Old Town. Open daily from 9am to 12pm. The beer is good and you will enjoy the traditional Bavarian oompah bands. They have their own beer called HB beer. Free to enter but often too crowded to enter. The ground floor is the main hall.

The menu at the Hofbrauhaus includes sausages, pork knuckle, sauerkraut and potatoes, and grilled chicken. I will highlight the HB menu because it is most representative of typical Bavarian food and drink. The prices are higher than most places.

The Hofbrauhaus produces their own beer called HB. The HB dark is 7.60E per litre. HB original is my favorite. This beer is a lighter blonde beer at 7.60E litre. Then there is Weisse beer which is a wheat beer unpurified.

The food menu starts with:

Bratzeit plate of cold cuts and cheeses ....9.90E.
Munich sausage salad 6.90
Popular potato soup 3.50
Brockwurst and potato salad 6.50
Two original Veal sausages............................... 4.90
Two white sausages with potato salad 8.90
      —this is my favorite—
Bavarian meat loaf... 7.50
Knuckle of pork (Bavarians love this) 10.50
Suckling pig 11.90
Half Chicken 9.50
Weiner Schnitzel (veal)................................. 17.90
Brewmaster Steak.. 8.90
Apple strudel (to finish) 6.90

What a variety!

The Duke of Bavaria, Wilhelm V. founded the Hofbrauhaus in 1589. It was founded as the Royal brewery to the Duke's Residence, which is nearby. It had to be rebuilt after WWII. The beer hall can serve 3,500 guests. 120 tables are reserved for regular guests. There is an outside beergarden where guests meet in the summer to experience the beergarden atmosphere.

The exact address for the Hofbrauhaus is Platzl 9, 80331 Munchen. Tel +49 (0)89-29 0136-100. Fax. +49 (0) 89-29 0136-129. hbteam@hofbraeuhaus.de. www.hofbrauhaus.de. Have fun!

Next, visit St. Michael's Church in Marienplatz. Here you find the largest barrel vault in the city. The style is Baroque. It is the final resting place of King Ludwig II, the mad king. Church entry is free.

Frauenkirche with its easily recognizable twin onion domes is next on the list to visit. The domes are the symbol of the city. This church is called the Church of Our Lady. It was built in the 15th century in Gothic style. Much of the church was bombed by the allies in WWII, but was rebuilt.

There is much to choose from for sightseeing in Munich. Other suggested sites are the Deutsches Museum, great for science lovers. Be sure to see the transportation section. Other recommendations are the Schloss Nymphenburg. This is a Baroque castle which served as a summer home for Bavarian rulers. Constructed in 1664, it includes a park of 500 acres. Be sure to see the collection of carriages.

Stop off to see the English Gardens. This is the largest urban park in Germany. There is a beergarden. A great place to relax.

Next see the Residence Museum. This was the official in-town home of the royal family. Be sure to see the fabulous collection of jewelry, silver and gold. You can take the tram back to Marienplatz.

After visiting the Hofbrauhaus, you may visit the nearby Viktualien market. The market was founded in 1807 by the Bavarian King. This is Munich's open air market. A great place to buy picnic supplies such as breads, cheese, fruit, and vegetables. Spicy meatloaf is popular. Great for snacks. There is a small beergarden. Open Monday-Saturdays. The market is located behind St. Peters near Marienplatz. Don't forget to see the huge maypole. Check it out!

While visiting Marienplatz, visit the beautiful churches. The oldest parish church is St. Peter's Church. The church was built in the 13th century. The interior is literally covered with gold. If you have the stamina you can climb the 302 steps to the top for a panoramic view of the city.

It is possible to visit a museum for free. Most museums in Munich have an admission fee. The city museums are free every Sunday. For example, the Municipal Museum is free. It gives you an overview of the history of the city and daily life.

Shopping.

Souvenirs are plentiful in Munich especially in the pedestrian zone on Neuhauser Old Town before you reach the Rathaus. There are numerous shops with Bavarian souvenirs. My favorite is the Shop Max Krug. It is your best stop for Black Forest Cuckoo clocks, Beer steins, Nutcrackers, and porcelans. I have never seen so many beer steins! They offer worldwide shipping. The address is Max Krug, Neuhauser Strasse 2, 80331 Munich. Tel +49 89 23 2698 70. info@max_krug.com

Little Bavaria Shop offers a wide variety of souvenirs representative of Bavaria. It is "The Brand Store in Munich. www.little-bavaria.de. Located on Orlandostrasse 2, D-80331 Munchen. Tel (0049) 89 260 10177. shop@ little-bavaria.de

Some shoppers prefer department stores which also offer clothing. Karstadt is the top of the line, C&A, and HM are popular as well. Beck's is also an upscale store.

Bavaria.

Now it is time to leave Munich and explore the splendid sights of the countryside of Bavaria. Since I am an independent traveler, I selected Viator Tours to see Bavaria by taking a series of ten hour bus day tours. This was an excellent choice. We departed daily outside the Karstadt Department Store, opposite the train station, at 8am. That was one reason to choose Hotel Litty which is only two blocks south. You can contact Viator Tours at 1-866-648-5873 or 1-888-651-9785 in USA. International 1 (702) 648-5873 or Viator.com to view their tours. Just select the country, region, or city. It is easy to use and book. They offer a free newsletter.

I scheduled three day trips with Viator. First, King Ludwig II dream castles of Neuschwanstein and Lindenhof. Next the Romantic Road to visit the small towns of Rothenberg and Harburg. Finally, Berchtesgaden and Eagles Nest, Hitlers mountain retreat near the Austrian border.

The cost for a single tour was:

Ludwig Castles 59.90 USD
Romantic Road 57.46 USD
Eagles Nest 57.46 USD

King Ludwig's Castles:

Schloss Neuschwanstein was built by King Ludwig II (the mad king) from 1869 to 1886. The castle is called the "Fairy Tale" castle and was the dream castle of Ludwig. It was the model for Disney's Sleeping Beauty Castle. The castle was constructed in the style of a medieval fortress. It was built on a cliff overlooking a ravine with a breathtaking view of the mountains. This castle is a must see and was the highlight of my Munich Bavaria trip.

Visitors to Neuschwanstein are placed into groups of sixty sightseers for a thirty minute tour. Originally the architects had planned on having 200 rooms. But the castle was not completed and only 15 rooms and halls were finished.

The largest room of the palace is the Hall of the Singers. The Throne room is next in size or floor space. It is located in the west wing of the Palace and occupies the third and fourth floors. An "apse" was constructed to contain Ludwig's throne but the throne itself was never completed.

The Throne room is the most impressive room. With the "apse" it reminds you of a church interior. Actually it is said that Ludwig wanted "to pay homage to royalty as given by the grace of God." The area was surrounded by paintings of Jesus, The Twelve Apostles, and canonized kings. Notice the mosaic floor, most impressive. The large chandelier is most impressive. It is made of gold plated brass. It is an example of Ludwig's lesson in extravagance. As much "glitz" as possible.

To reach Neuschwanstein Castle you will need to travel to the town of Hohenschwangau. I took the Viator bus tour. But if you are traveling by train from Munich, you will arrive first in Fussen and then take the local bus to Hohenschwangau. Here you find a ticket office to enter the castle.

To get to the castle you can walk up a steep hill, take horse drawn carriage or a transfer bus. Either way you will need to walk up the final part of the way. At some point you might walk to the Marien bridge to take the best photo of the castle.

Crowds can be large. The wait can be long. But eventually you will get there. Some 6000 visitors tour the castle daily during the summer.

If you have time while in Hohenschwangau town, visit the Museum of Bavarian King's. Then you can admire the original coat of King Ludwig II. It faces the beautiful waterfront of Lake Alpsee and is just a short walk up from Hotel Muller.

The bus tour with Viator continues next to Linderhof Palace in Southwest Bavaria. This palace was also constructed by King Ludwig II and the only one which he lived to see completed. Lindenhof was constructed between 1870-1878 in the French rococo style. Ludwig II admired Versailles and Louis XIV.

When entering Lindenhof you will be immediately impressed by the ceiling of gold depicting the French Sun King, Louis XVI. Ludwig liked to identify with the French Sun King. In the middle of the entrance hall is a statue of Louis XIV on horseback. Ludwig used Lindenhof more as a private residence where he could get away and enjoy peace and seclusion.

The most elaborate room in the Lindenhof Castle is the Hall of Mirrors. Mirrors framed in white and gold are located on the walls surrounding the room. The chandeliers are made of ivory. Ludwig used this as a sitting room and often would spend the entire night in the room. He enjoyed the illusion created by the mirrors.

How did King Ludwig II die? His body was found in Lake Starnberg on June 13, 1886. The body of his psychiatrist was also discovered. The real cause of King Ludwig's death has been a mystery ever since. There are two conspiracy theories. Was it suicide by drowning? Or was it murder to rid the politicians of this eccentric king? We may never know the truth.

After leaving Lindenhof, Viator tours will make a short shopping stop in Oberammergau, The home of the famous Passion Play.

Oberammergau is also noted for its fairy tale painted Bavarian homes. Each depicts a biblical scene or fairy tale characters, such as the "big bad wolf."

For shopping, stop by the shop by Barbara Heinzeller. She sells Cuckoo Clocks and authentic Bavarian woodcarvings. The shop is located near the downtown at Theaterstr 14, 82487, Oberammergau, across from the passion play theatre. Phone +49 (0) 8822-4663, Fax +49 (0) 8822-4584. www.barbara-heinzeller.de. Take a short walk to the middle of town. The people are friendly.

Harburg and Rothenberg. Romantic Road.

My next tour with Viator took me from Munich along the Romantic Road. The Romantic Road stretches from Wurzburg to Fussen. It is Germany's most popular tourist routes because of its coverage of Medieval towns, villages, castles, and churches.

Our first stop was Harburg. Sitting high on a hill and overlooking the town is the impressive authentic medieval

Harburg Castle. It was bult in 1150 and was not damaged in WWII. It is a true representation of the middle ages without the "glitz" of some other castles. It is the best preserved medieval castle in Germany. It is what a real castle looks like.

Tours are available at regular intervals in German and English. The castle complex includes a castle house and a chapel. It is surrounded by a wall and six towers. In the courtyard there is a well for water.

The castle has hotel rooms located in the towers and a small restaurant on the premises. There are exhibits of weapons and a dungeon. The address is 86655 Harburg, Bavaria, Germany. +49 (0) 90 80 96 860. Email www.stadt-harburg-schwaben.de.

Rothenburg.

The city is a quaint well-preserved medieval city with town walls and cobbled stone streets. A great town for walking and shopping. The history of Rothenburg started in the 10th century when a castle was built at the southern end of the village. It is one of the foremost well-preserved medieval villages. A must see!

The town hall and market square is the center of life inside the city walls. The town hall tower offers the best view of the town. It is surrounded by shops and cafes.

St. Jacob's Church is another famous landmark in the town. It was built in 1336 and has many treasures of antiquity. Be sure to view the 600 year old stained glass window.

For lunch I selected the Ratsstube at market place 6, just across from the market square central. A true Bavarian tavern atmosphere. I selected the sliced pork in mushroom sauce as my main course at 9.50E and a glass of red wine. They also offer:

Fish..10.00E
Potato Soup 3.50
Meatloaf..8.00
Deer Goulash...14.00

The address is marketplatz 6, 91541, Rothenburg, Bavaria. Tel 09861-5511. The price range is moderate.

A popular pastry snack is the Schneeball. It is similar to a doughnut and in English is called a snowball. It is pastry strips shaped like a ball and fried. A great place for the schneeball is the Café UHL. Just inside the city gate at Plonlein 8, 91541 Rothenburg. Tel 098 61-4895. www. hotel-uhl.de. They also offer many other pastries. A great place for a snack when walking around.

I did not stay overnight in Rothenburg but many people recommended the Burg Hotel. The rooms range from $125.00 in the off season. It is located in a 12th century building overlooking the Tauber Valley. The address is Klostergasse 1-3, Rothenburg 91541.

For shopping I recommend the shop of Anneliese Friese at Gruner Markt 7-8 near the Rathaus, Rothenburg, 91541. Tel. 0961/7166. This is the home of the authentic Cuckoo Clock. Also beer steins, maps, paintings, porcelain, and glassware.

Rothenburg is known for its original Christmas ornaments and hand-made toys. The best shop for this is Katie Wohlfahtl's Christmas Ornament Shop. They have more Christmas ornaments under one roof than anywhere else. They can even ship them home.

It was time to leave this charming medieval town. Traveling with Viator tours, we returned to Munich. What a beautiful day on the Romantic Road in Bavaria!

Berchtesgaden and Eagle's Nest. Today with Viator Tours I visit Hitler's famous mountain retreat in far south Bavaria.

Kehlsteinhaus is the German word for Eagle's Nest perched 6,017 feet atop the mountain just outside Obersalzberg, formerly Hitler's Bavarian home and southern headquarters of the Nazi government. It is only 12 miles from Salzburg, Austria.

The Eagle's Nest is a mountain chalet which was given to Hitler on his 50th birthday in 1939 by Martin Bormann and the inner circle of the party. Hitler used it as a holiday retreat and to greet diplomats. Today it is a restaurant and open to visitors. It is considered an engineering feat. The view from the top is spectacular. On a clear day you can see Salzburg. There are also fantastic views of the village of Berchtesgaden and the river valley below. A combination of a bus ride and elevator takes the visitor to the top. It is a piece of history with amazing views. The trip to Eagle's Nest was the highlight of my German trip!

It is said that Hitler rarely visited Eagle's Nest because he suffered from vertigo. Eva Braun enjoyed Eagle's Nest and was mostly responsible for prompting Hitler to visit there. It is normally open from May through October. The address is Kehlsteinhaus, 83471 Bertesgaden, Bavaria, Germany. 08652 2969.

Eagle's Nest historical tours is highly recommended if you arrive and need a tour. It is conducted by professional guides who speak fluent English. You can make reservations at Konigsseer Strasse 2, 83471 Berchtesgaden, Germany. Tel +49 652 64971. They also offer a Sound of Music Tour.

Today the Eagle's Nest Chalet is a very good restaurant with outdoor seating for dining and a beer garden. Indoor seating is also available. I preferred the outdoor. The weather was pleasant and the view terrific. It was great to enjoy a good German HB beer at the top in the company of many German tourists.

Be sure to see the historic fireplace inside the chalet. The red Italian marble was donated by Mussolini. Many U.S. soldiers took a piece of the marble home as a souvenir.

I decided to dine at the Kehlsteinhaus terrace beergarden on the patio. It was a lovely day for being outdoors. I shared a table with German tourists. My beer was the HB or Hofbrauhaus Munchen. A litre was E3.80. For lunch I ordered "Schnitzel Wiener Art," or breaded pork cutlet with French fries at E12.90. Excellent choice! It is a great place to relax and enjoy the view.

Other dishes on the menu were:

```
Open ham sandwich ....................................7.30E
Bockwurst with potato salad ........................7.10E
Big Bowl salad...............................................9.30E
Cheese Board ...............................................6.30E
Wine.............................................................4.60E
Coffee ..........................................................3.90E
```

When you get off the bus on the way up, take some time to visit the documentation center. It is a small museum or archives designed so Germans can learn and understand their recent history, i.e., the Nazi past. If you have time you can explore the vast bunker system beneath the museum.

Why visit Munich and Bavaria? It is simple. Because of the wealth of tourist options available in this city and federal state. There are many choices available depending upon your interest and time available. Planning is essential.

Munich is known for its history, architecture, museums, churches, markets, opera, science and education, and its festive atmosphere during Octoberfest. For me, it was the history.

The Alps are just one hour away. There you find the traditional Bavarian culture, the image of the "Lederhosin," and people drinking beer. It represents the folklore and age old traditions. Bavaria is Germany's most popular tourist destination.

Bavaria is the home of "mad" King Ludwig's castles. Most popular is Neuschwanstein Castle. Ludwig's other favorite castle was Linderhof Castle.

Finish your trip to Bavaria by visiting Berchtesgaden and Eagle's Nest. At the top of the mountain enjoy the view of the valley below.

Of course, don't forget the Romantic Road and visits to medieval walled cities and castles, Harburg and Rothenburg.

As you can see, there are many things to see and do. Make your choices and do your planning. Just Go!

26

Peru: Machu Picchu Adventure

"Travel makes one modest. You see what a tiny
place you occupy in the world."
—Gustave Flaubert

Machu Picchu, the lost city of the Incas, is located
in the Cuzco Region of Peru. The Incas started
building the city circa AD 1400. Work was abandoned
and restarted in 1438. In 1450, at the height of the Incan
Empire, it was completed. It was abandoned again in 1572
during the Spanish conquest of Francisco Pizarro. Today, it
is a World Heritage Site and is considered to be one of the
New Seven Wonders of the World.

The Spanish conquistadores did not find Machu
Picchu, the greatest secret of the Incas. Because the Incas
built it so high in the clouds, the Spanish never found it.
The city was also hidden from eyesight because it was far
above the ridge of the mountain. Machu Picchu is one of
the most spectacular regions and is 7,970 feet above sea
level. The Urubamba Valley lies below. The popular theory
is Machu Picchu was built in dedication to the Incan
Emperor, Puchacuti, "He who shapes the Earth." He made
Cuzco an empire and ruled from 1438.

I arrived in Cuzco by way of Lima. I made the colonial city of Cuzco my base camp to explore Machu Picchu. My trip to Cuzco was a day trip by train. I arrived in Aguas Calientes and took a tourist bus up the winding road to the granite ruins of Machu Picchu. There was a hotel or lodge at the top where we had lunch. I would recommend sleeping there at least one night. Just being there is a mystical feeling. You could stay in the lodge or one of the numerous hotels in Aguas Calientes. This way your sightseeing will be more relaxing. Most any travel tour company can arrange this for you.

Altitude sickness can be a problem. You will need to become accustomed to the altitude. On the first day, take it slow and don't be too active. In the cafés and hotels, you can find cocoa tea. Drinking cocoa tea leaves is a good remedy for altitude sickness. The altitude in Cuzco is 11,000 feet. A stay in Cuzco should prepare you for Machu Picchu.

The winding highway up the mountain, which connects Agua Calientes with Machu Picchu, is named the Hiram Bingham Highway. It is used by the tour buses. Hiram Bingham was a citizen of the US and a Yale historian who first brought the attention of the world to Machu Picchu in 1911. A local farmer who knew of its existence led Hiram Bingham to the Machu Picchu site. It is no longer the "lost city of the Incas." It is now an important tourist attraction. Machu Picchu was built in the classical Incan style. The buildings are constructed of carefully placed stones cut to fit together tightly. The Incas were masters of stone construction. We are not sure of its purpose. Was it a ceremonial city or a sacred site dedicated to the Incan Emperor?

The essentials for a visit to Machu Picchu are the Temple of the Sun, the Temple of the Three Windows, and

Intihuatana. Crowds in the summer can be large, and you will need to move quickly between the sites. The ruins are open from dawn to dusk.

The Temple of the Sun is a good example of Incan stonework. The large stones fit perfectly together without mortar. Inti, the sun god, was the greatest deity of the Incas. In the mornings, the sun's rays illuminate the stone in the center of the temple.

The Temple of the Three Windows is the main ceremonial area. It is also known for its stonework. The windows are in the shape of trapezoids. It is amazing how these many angled stones were fitted together by the Incas. This is one temple you will not forget.

Intihuatana, also called the hitching post of the sun, is believed to be an astronomic clock or calendar by the Incas. It is a sun dial carved of stone. The stones are arranged to point at the sun during the winter solstice.

Part of my visit to Peru included time in Lima, the capital of Peru. Lima was founded in 1535 by Francisco Pizarro, the Spanish conquistador. The Spanish ruled Peru for three hundred years. Today Lima is a mixture of the modern and colonial. If you miss Lima, you will miss a lot.

My hotel choice in Lima was the Gran Hotel Bolivar, once the best hotel in Lima. Now it is a three-star hotel, priced at fifty dollars per person. It was built in the 1920s on the Plaza San Martin. It is a nostalgic treat. The rooms are spacious in the old tradition. If you are seeking the romance of a different era, you will not be disappointed.

The Gran Hotel Bolivar overlooks the Plaza San Martín in El Centro. Because I was a student of Latin American history, I was overwhelmed by my view of the plaza from my hotel window. The plaza was built in 1921. At the center is a monument to José de San Martín, the South American liberator.

Today many tourists elect to stay in modern Miraflores, which is safer, quieter, and has more nightlife and shopping. The Miraflores Park Hotel is a good choice here. Many rooms have views of the Pacific Ocean. Within walking distance are a number of bars and restaurants. The hotel is expensive compared to the Bolivar, but there is a swimming pool on top of the hotel.

In colonial Lima is located Lima Centro, a good starting place for sightseeing. It is also called Plaza de Armas or Plaza Mayor. It is the center of Lima, founded by Pizarro. On the north side is the Presidential Palace, and nearby on the plaza, is the Municipalidad de Lima, or city hall.

Across the square is the cathedral. It has been reconstructed after earthquakes. The cathedral was first built in 1555. Pizarro's body lies in the chapel.

The Cathedral of San Francisco is the best example of colonial churches in Lima. The ceramic tiles are from Seville. There are carved ceilings overhead. Religious art is a favorite with visitors. The catacombs are another special feature.

I especially liked the Museo de Oro, or the Gold Museum. There I found a vast array of gold objects and jewelry from pre-Incan times. There are vases, ear flaps, earrings, brooches, gold pendants, and the famous *tumi*, the ceremonial knife, used in burial ceremonies. The ancient Peruvian people were experts working with metals. There are also silver artifacts. The address is Avenida Alonso de Molina 1100.

The Museo de la Nation, or National Museum, is a nice, big museum, giving you a good overview of Peruvian history. This is an important stop for those going on to further explore Peru. The museum gives you a historical background for your Peruvian trip. It is in four levels. The ceramic exhibition is popular. You will see replicas of the main archaeological sites of Peru. Plus, there are paintings. It is located at Javier Prado Este, Avenida Nº 2465, San Borja.

Next stop on the museum tour should be the Museo Archaeologico Rafael Larco Herrera, or the Museum of Archaeology, Anthropology, and History. The museum was founded in 1926 in an old mansion built in 1707. This museum houses the largest private collection of pre-Columbian art that exists in the world. On exhibit are ceramics, gold, stone, wood, and textiles. There is even a vault gold room. The museum is located on Bolivar Avenida Nº 1515, Pueblo Libre.

There are other museums, but the museums above should give the traveler a complete picture of the Peruvian past in archaeology, history, and art.

A visit to Lima is not complete unless you sample the food. There are excellent restaurants offering a variety of foods for all budgets. The popular dish is ceviche, or raw fish served with onion, potato, chili peppers, and toasted corn, all marinated in lime or lemon juice. The national drink is Pisco sour.

The gateway to Machu Picchu is the ancient Incan city of Cuzco, a city most tourists will visit on their way to Machu Picchu. Cuzco was the capital of the Incan Empire and was also the home of the Quechua Indian culture. It is a beautiful city with well-preserved colonial architecture and Incan stonework. It is the center of the Quechua culture in the Andes and a mixture of Incan and Spanish history.

The central area of Cuzco is the Plaza de Armas. This is the focal point, and most of Cuzco can be seen on foot. The

Plaza de Armas contains parts of the original stone walls. Plus, the plaza has two colonial churches. There are also shops and restaurants.

If you have more interest in Inca stone walls, you can trek northwest from the Plaza de Armas to Sacsayhuanan, thought to be an Incan religious site. These are the closest Incan ruins to Cuzco. It is best to use a guide. The outer walls have survived. In the style of Incan workmanship, the wall of stones fit together perfectly without the use of mortar. A battle at this site by the Spanish and Incas in 1536 caused the deaths of thousands of Incas.

Cuzco is the popular place to stay before going to Machu Picchu. By train, it is sixty-nine miles to Machu Picchu. My visit to Peru was an exciting look into the history of Incan culture and the Spanish colonization. Tourists have a fascination with Machu Picchu and the Incan ruins, which cannot be found anywhere else on earth. Peru is an archaeological treasure chest.

27

Prague: The Essentials

"Travel is like a great blank canvas, and the
painting on the canvas is only limited by one's
imagination."
—Ross Morley

Prague, the capital of the Czech Republic, has been a
popular tourist destination since the fall of the Iron
Curtain. Prague is rich in history, culture, and architecture.
Prague suffered less damage during World War II, making
it possible to see its historic architecture in its original
form. Today the historic center of Prague is included in the
UNESCO list of world heritage sites.

My visit to Prague took place during one of my spring
breaks while I was teaching. Therefore, I will just try to
cover the essentials. I did mostly walking tours. It is an easy
city for walking. There is much to see and do. One can also
take the tram.

Prague, like most major European cities, offers a wide
range of hotel possibilities at various price levels. I selected
the Hotel Opera because of its old-world charm and central
location to historic buildings. From the opera, you have

easy walking distance to Old Town Square. Of course, you can take the tram; there is a tram stop in front of the hotel.

My stay at the Hotel Opera was prior to its renovation. When I was there, the price for a standard single was fifty US dollars. I am sure it is more expensive today.

A walking tour should include a visit to St. Vitus Cathedral and the thousand-year-old Prague Castle. Old Town Square, with its astronomical clock, is a must see. Take a walk across the romantic Charles Bridge.

The main sightseeing areas of Prague are separated by the Vitara River. On the left bank there is the Prague Castle area and Lesser Town. The right bank is home to Old Town. The beautiful Charles Bridge spans the Vitara River and connects Old Town and Lesser Town.

The heart of Prague's historical center is Old Town Square. Old Town City Hall is located here and was built in 1338. Prague dates from 880 with the founding of the castle. On the outside of city hall is the famous Old Town astronomical clock. The clock shows, by the hour, a display of the twelve apostles. Also in Old Town, you will find the Tyn Cathedral with its Gothic spheres. It towers over Old Town Square.

You will not regret a climb to the top of the tower of Old Town Hall. It offers a panoramic view of the square and beyond. There are sidewalk cafes and coffee shops in the square.

Continue your walk toward the Vitara River and the Charles Bridge. The construction of the stone bridge was commissioned by Czech King and Holy Roman Charles IV in 1357. There is a tower standing on each end of the bridge. Baroque statues are placed along either side of the Charles Bridge. Charles Bridge is on the top of every Prague visitor's must see list.

Next stop is the Prague Castle, with the St. Vitus Cathedral, which stores the Czech Crown Jewels. From the castle you will get a beautiful view of Prague and the Vitara River. The Prague Castle experienced one of its greatest periods during the reign of Charles IV when it became the seat of the Holy Roman Empire. It is not a single castle, but a series of buildings and churches. It also houses several museums including the National Gallery. Today it is the seat of the Head of State of the New Czech Republic.

As you walk through Old Town you will see many restaurants, cafés, bars, and pubs. Some of the well-known dishes of Czech cuisine are pork with cabbage and dumplings, sausage with dumplings, and beef or schnitzel. A good dinner must be accompanied by the Czech national drink—beer. The Czechs produce famous pilsner beers such as Pilsner Urquell or Budweiser. Yes, the Czechs produced the first Budweiser and refuse to sell out to the US's Budweiser.

Prague has become one of Europe's most popular tourist destinations. It is a city rich in culture and history. It has bridges, cathedrals, gold-tipped towers, church domes, and a certain old-world charm. Prague has more than ten major museums. In modern times, it is a vibrant city full of energy, music, and cultural art. It is a city not to be missed in your tour of Europe.

28

Costa Rica: Rain forests, Mountains, and Beaches

"Through travel I first became aware of the
outside world; it was through travel that
I found my own introspective way into
becoming a part of it."
—Eudora Welty

Most visitors to Costa Rica consider it one of the most beautiful places on the planet. People come here for nature and the environment. Costa Rica offers rain forests, mountains, and beaches to explore. The people are exceptionally friendly. *Pura vida* is the popular Spanish term used by locals to describe life in Costa Rica. Translated, it means "Life is good."

I started my trip in the urban center of San José. The city was founded by the Spanish in 1737. The coffee boom stimulated the growth of the city. San José is usually a temporary stop prior to visiting the rain forest or beaches. But it is worthwhile to spend time there on the way in or out of the country.

My hotel in San José was the Hotel Balmoral, located in the center of the city. A single room was sixty dollars per night, which included a buffet breakfast served at the top floor. The rooms were clean and had AC and TV. There is a restaurant and bar downstairs. It is located on Avenida Central, Calle 7 & 9.

Across the street is the Hotel Presidente. Rates are slightly higher than at the Balmoral. It has an outdoor patio and restaurant and is convenient to the main historical and cultural landmark of San José.

Down the street, just off the plaza, is the historic Gran Hotel Costa Rica. There is a twenty-four-hour casino on the ground floor. Room rates are sixty-four to eighty-four dollars US dollars. The location is Calle 3 and 2 Avenida Central. The hotel dates from the 1930s. The patio café is popular, a great place to have coffee or a drink and watch the passing parade of people. It is directly across from the Teatro Nacional.

Just south of Avenida Central on Avenida 1 is my favorite bar and restaurant, El Trabajor, or the Workers. They offer cheap Imperial *cerveza* and typical Costa Rican food, such as bicsteak. They also offer *mariscos*, or seafood. A visit here offers the opportunity to meet the local, everyday citizens.

Teatro Nacional is considered the most outstanding example of architecture in San José. It is modeled on the Palais Garnier, the Paris opera house. It was built in 1897 after a famous Paris opera singer bypassed San José on her tour. The tour of the museum includes paintings and statues. It is located directly across the street from the Gran Hotel. The Teatro Nacional is a must see in San José. The financing of the Teatro Nacional came from a tax on coffee exports. The people of Costa Rica were determined an opera star would not skip over them again.

A must see in the Teatro Nacional is the huge canvas painting showing the coffee harvest and export. Nearby is the Museo del Oro, or Museum of gold. Pre-Columbian ancient gold is shown as a collection. There is also a coin collection.

Another important museum to visit is the Museo Nacional, located toward the west of the bus station at Calle 17, Avenida Central and 2. It is housed in the old army headquarters. This museum displays archaeological items and historical artifacts.

For one-stop shopping, I recommend La Casona, Calle Central, Ave Central and 1. It is a multi-level large complex of many shop stalls that sell handicrafts by artisans from all over Costa Rica. Be sure to bargain.

Leaving the city and getting out into the countryside is the reason tourists come to Costa Rica. It is one of the most bio diverse places on earth. For my internal travel in Costa Rica, I used Costa Rica Expeditions. One advantage is that they take care of the transportation, whether by small plane or by jeep or by van. They do the planning and supply the guides. I have traveled to Costa Rica five different times.

One of my favorite places to visit is the Corcovado Rain Forest and Beach. There's a tented camp there called the Laleona Lodge. The tents are just above the beach and have porches facing the ocean. The jungle is behind the tent.

It is a one-hour flight by small Cessna aircraft to Corcovado. The landing strip is on the beach. You then walk on the beach to your tent or lodge.

Activities include a trek into the Corcovado Park. It is one of the most biologically diverse rain forests in Central America. It is exciting to see Amazon Parrots. Also, you will see several species of snakes and perhaps poison dart frogs. It is indeed an exotic location. I love the night sounds from the rainforest. Fishing and night hikes are optional. Of course, there is leisure time on the beach.

Another favorite tour of mine is to visit the town of Monte Verde and the adjacent cloud forest reserve. It is called a cloud forest because it is at the top of a mountain. The town was founded by Quakers who settled there to find religious sanctuary after World War II. It is located in northwestern Costa Rica. The town is named Santa Elena.

The Monteverde Lodge was my hotel in Monteverde. It is a short trek to the cloud forest and the tour of Santa Elena. It is a great location for hiking, bird watching, viewing wildlife, and horseback riding. The rooms have a garden view or view of the forest. The grounds include a short trail which leads to an observation platform.

The popular tour to take is with a guide to follow a walking trail in the rainforest. Most of the trails are very muddy. You can rent rubber boots at the entrance or bring your own for a better fit. Hikers meet at the Hummingbird building to see a slideshow and receive an orientation. From here, they can take a two-and-a-half-hour trek. The guides speak English. Everyone hopes to see a quetzal. Most often you will see a golden toad. Hummingbirds are easily spotted.

Other options near Santa Elena are the butterfly garden, the canopy tour, or the cheese factory, which was founded by the Quakers. Monteverde is in one of the most interesting places in Costa Rica.

My next most interesting place to visit is Tortuga Lodge, located in Costa Rica's northeast Caribbean coast, in the Tortuguero River. From San José you can take a small Cessna plane or a combination of a van and boat ride.

Tortuguero National Park is one of the largest protected areas of the tropical rainforest in Central America. The marine area is the most important breeding ground for the green sea turtle. The beaches are not suitable for swimming because the surf is too rough and the current is strong.

The best way to explore the park is by a boat with your guide. By boat, you may view various species of monkeys such as the spider or howler monkeys. You can also see sloths and raccoons often. There are also iguanas and dart frogs. There are over three hundred species of birds, including parrots and toucans. It is a wonderland.

My next stop in Costa Rica is on the central Pacific coast at Quepos and Manuel Antonio National Park. This is south of the beach town of Jaco, which is popular with people from San José and is known as a party beach and surfing beach. South of Jaco is Quepos known for game fishing and the gateway to Manuel Antonio National Park. Quepos is about a hundred miles from San José. It is on the central Pacific coast. There is a small airport and bus service.

My hotel in Quepos was the Hotel Tres Banderas. The owners and managers are English-speaking Europeans. It is located just off the main road from Quepos to Manuel Antonio National Park. It is a nice hotel and well managed by the owners who live on the property. It is quiet and relaxing in its tropical environment. The hotel has a swimming pool. The mailing address is P.O. Box 258-6350 Quepos. Banderas@rasca.co.cr. The price range is moderate to high.

The major reason for visiting Quepos is to tour the Manuel Antonio National Park. It was declared a national park in 1972. Camping is not allowed in the park. It is popular because of its beaches, tropical forests, and walking trails.

Some people tour the park to see the wildlife. Monkeys abound in the park. Sloths and raccoons are easily seen as well. There are over three hundred fifty species of birds in the park. There are toucans and scarlet macaws. This is one of the most visited parks in Costa Rica. For environmental purposes, the park is closed on Mondays.

Big game fishing is popular in Quepos. There is a variety of fish. The sailfish and billfish are popular. Organized fishing trips are easily arranged in the marinas of Quepos or at your hotel. Organized tours are easily arranged. There is trail hiking, canopy tours, rafting, bird watching, horseback riding, and kayaking. Again, your hotel can arrange these for you. The Hacienda Baru, a private nature reserve, can also make arrangements.

After touring Quepos, I flew back to San José and stayed in the Balmoral Hotel.

I am always impressed by Costa Rica's diversity and respect for the environment. Costa Rica has diverse landscapes, flora, and fauna. With rainforests, volcanoes, beaches, high mountains, and dry, tropical, and temperate forests, it is a paradise for environmentalists and nature lovers.

29

Madagascar: An Island and a Country

"The more you travel,
the less you realize you know."
—Anthony Bourdain

Madagascar is located some 250 miles off the east coast of Africa in the Indian Ocean. I flew there from Johannesburg, South Africa. It is separated from Africa by the Mozambique Channel and is south of the equator. It is the world's fourth largest island. (Greenland is the largest.) It has a tropical climate. The island was separated from the mainland of Africa some 165 million years ago. Madagascar is a naturalist's paradise because most of the plants and animals are unique to the island. Tourists travel here to see and photograph the lemur.

The first Europeans to arrive in Madagascar were the Portuguese in 1500. But there seems to be an Indonesian origin of the Malagasy people because it is reflected in their spoken language. Also the French left a lasting influence. In 1883, the French attacked and occupied the major seaports. Madagascar became a French protectorate. But the British invaded in World War II and freed the island from Vichy France. Finally in 1960, Madagascar achieved full independence. The French language still has a strong place in their society.

Most people travel to Madagascar because of its natural history. It is an island country where some animals and plants cannot be found anywhere else. Examples are the primates called lemurs and the huge baobab trees.

By plane, people arrive at the Irato Airport at Antananarivo on Tana. It is the capital of Madagascar, located in the central highlands. Most people stay only a day or so in Tana. My hotel in Tana was the Tana Plaza Hotel on the popular Avenue de Independence. It is an upper level hotel in price range with a good location and atmosphere. Also, a recommended hotel is the Hotel Colbert on Rue Rat Simamanga, which is often full. It has excellent food. New hotels and restaurants are opening all the time in Taa.

Safety is a factor to be considered in Tana. The gap between the rich and poor has caused a rise in crime against tourists, especially in Tana. Be careful with your valuables and be aware of your surroundings. Violent crime is rare, but g o to the police and file a report if you are robbed.

Tana is a good place to buy traditional handicrafts before setting out on your nature journey. You can buy just about every type of handicrafts, such as wood carvings, tablecloths, and much more. Semi-precious stones are also for sale.

Departing from Tana, I had my own guide and four-wheel-drive vehicle. The roads are often bumpy and dusty. You will need an experienced driver.

Our first destination was the Perinet Special Reserve, which protects the Indri family of lemurs. I used the local Perinet guides. They are the best in Madagascar because of their experience and knowledge. All the guides know where to find the lemurs so everyone can see lemurs and most also hear their singing-like sound—an experience to remember.

There are twenty-three species of lemurs. It is exciting to see them leap from tree to tree or listen to them sing as they call to each other in the tree tops. Night walks are optional. A word of warning: the walks are often over muddy trails. Dress in appropriate footwear. The sightseeing walks are considered easy to moderate in difficulty.

My next stop was the Berenty Private Reserve Plantation. To get there, we drove through the "spiny desert" habitat of Berenty. As we entered the spiny forest, we saw the large trunks of the baobab trees. The spiny tree is called the octopus tree and looks similar to cactus. The branches contain thorns. They are masses of branches and thorns.

Berenty is an excellent place to see the ring-tailed lemurs and the acrobatic sifaka lemur. The sifaka are noted for the sideways hops they use to get around on the ground. They are friendly and not shy.

Berenty is a small private park, which borders on the Mandrare River. The forest trails are broad and not muddy. Bird watching is also popular. The park has overnight accommodations.

A trip to Madagascar would not be complete without seeing baobab trees. Just north of Morondava is the famous Avenue of the Baobab Trees. It is a unique grove of more than a dozen trees. Some of the trees are over eight hundred years old.

There are six native species of the baobab tree in Madagascar. The baobab is often called the upside down tree and the monkey bread tree. The tree can grow as tall as one hundred feet and have a trunk diameter of forty feet or more.

The trunk of the tree looks swollen because this is where water is stored. They grow primarily in the southwest region, which is arid. The baobab is deciduous which means it sheds its leaves in the dry season. The Malagasy people consider the baobab tree to be sacred.

Madagascar is a place I will always remember. It has a stunning diversity of plant and animal species found nowhere else in the world. Animal and plants long gone from Africa have survived and thrived in Madagascar. It is a once in a lifetime natural history adventure.

30

The Dominican Republic: Paradise Found

"Adventure is worthwhile."
—Aristotle

Christopher Columbus discovered the Dominican Republic on his first voyage to the Americas in 1492. In the following year, the first permanent European settlement in the New World was founded, the city of Santo Domingo. It was the first capital of the New World. The first cathedral and the first castle in the Spanish traditions were built there.

The Dominican Republic is known for its white sandy beaches and its blue and turquoise ocean. Bavaro Beach at Punta Cana, with its beautiful palm trees, is one of the best in the Caribbean. It has the longest strip of white sand on the island, containing twenty-one miles of white sandy beach. The offshore coral reef makes swimming easy. The Latin culture causes the Dominican Republic to stand out from the other islands of the Caribbean. The island seems to move to the beat of merengue, the official music of the Dominican Republic.

The food is a gastronomic delight—a mixture of Spanish colonial and Caribbean. Grilled seafood is the most popular selection. Paella, accompanied by potatoes and salad, is also a popular choice. Also, shrimp and grilled calamari are excellent. Presidente beer flows freely, as does local red or white wine or Barceló rum. There is also Brugal rum.

La Bandera Dominicana is the official dish of the Dominican Republic. It's made up of meat, white rice, red beans, fried plantain, and salad. *Mangu*, boiled plantain with olive oil, is popular for breakfast or dinner.

All-inclusive resorts are the most popular hotels in the Dominican Republic. They are the best bargains. I elected to stay at the Barceló Dominican Beach Resort in Bavaro just north of the airport in Punta Cana. I flew there on Delta Airlines from Atlanta, a four-hour flight. The Barceló is an all-inclusive resort. You need no money while staying there. The Barceló group is owned by the Spanish in Baleaver España. They own several resorts in the Dominican Republic, Mexico, and Costa Rica. They are trying to give back to the community by adopting a local school, the El Salado School. The school is still in the process of rebuilding from the damage of Hurricane Georges.

The all-inclusive Barceló Resorts appeal to a variety of people, especially families, singles, and travelers of all ages because of the variety of activities. Whether it be learning to dance or taking Spanish lessons, there's something for everyone. The pools are beautiful. Also, on the Barceló premises is a sports bar and a casino. There are a variety of restaurants with live entertainment at night. The Barceló also has a disco. It's a very good value for the money. Check TripAdvisor for reviews.

The Barceló Dominican Beach Resort has nine restaurants and six bars. The Palmasol Restaurant is the main one for all three meals. There are restaurants featuring Mexican, Japanese, and Brazilian cuisines. Also, there is a beach bar and beach restaurant for lunch and dinner. The large pool has a swim-up bar. The Barceló rum flows freely. The Amigo Lobby Bar is popular all day long. Weddings can be arranged at the Barceló; one can use the beach or gazebo as the setting. Various ceremonies are available.

Punta Cana has several professional golf courses available to tourists. The beach is the main attraction, and you can freely stroll the beach, going from one resort to another. The beaches make for a relaxing vacation.

Organized events can be scheduled, such as sailing, fishing, snorkeling, diving, adventure trips, native tours, shopping, and day tours to Santo Domingo.

Shopping for handicrafts is popular. There are free shuttle buses from the Barceló to the Palma Real and San Juan shopping centers. Especially popular are the native stones of amber and larimar. The Dominican Republic is noted for its authentic amber, and larimar is a semi-precious stone native to the country. They both make beautiful necklaces. My favorite items to shop for are the colorful paintings. The variety of colors is amazing.

Wall canvas paintings are an exceptional value in the Dominican Republic. Just walk around the colonial zone in Santo Domingo or the beach at Bavaro. You can see many different works of art and paintings. There are many brightly colored paintings. Some of the paintings are from Haiti. Most are inexpensive if you bargain.

Cigars and rum are the things to take home for many visitors. Dominican rum and tobacco are considered to be the best in the world. Barceló and Brugal are the most famous brands of rum. The prices are better in grocery stores or small shops. La Silena in Santo Domingo is a large supermarket where you can buy anything. The souvenirs here are at a cheaper price.

Remember to always bargain over the price of handicrafts in the Dominican Republic. Most do not expect you to pay the first price. It never hurts to haggle. The Spanish phrase for "how much is it?" is "*cuanto es?*" "Less money, please" is "*Por favor, mas barato.*" "Expensive" is "*caro*". Go out and bargain!

Why travel to the Dominican Republic? I call it paradise found. The Dominican Republic has sugar white beaches, inexpensive resorts, and a showcase for nature that attracts tourists from all over the world. The hospitality of the people will impress you. The weather is perfect almost all year—except for hurricanes.

When Columbus first saw the Dominican Republic, he called it "the most beautiful island in the world." There is an array of activities to keep you busy, or you can have a relaxing, beach vacation. It is probably the most diverse destination in the Caribbean. The Dominican Republic is unforgettable. It is paradise found.

31

Hong Kong. Vibrant and Exciting

"Tell me and I will forget. Show
me and I will remember."
—Confucius

Upon your arrival in Hong Kong you sense an excitement you will not find anywhere else. The harbor is scenic and vibrant. It is a sight to be seen, especially at night with the brilliant lights. You can spend as much time as you choose traveling from the highs of Victoria Peak to Aberdeen, WanChai and then across the harbor on the Star Ferry to Kowloon and Nathan Street. National Geographic has named it one of the 50 places to visit in a lifetime. It is one of my favorite cities to visit. You seem to get caught up in the vibrancy of the city. The city is "open" twenty four hours. It never sleeps. More than likely you will arrive at the "New Airport" on LanTau Island west of Hong Kong. The airport is called Hong Kong International Airport at Chek LapKok, 25 miles from central Hong Kong. This new airport replaces the old airport in Kai Tak Kowloon which had the famous air approach close to the houses before landing. This had been one of the most exciting landings you would ever make. I have been to Hong Kong three times. My first two landings were at the old airport. The approach by airline was a thrill of a lifetime.

The easiest way to transfer to the city is by the MTR, or the mass transit railway. Cost is 90 HK dollars. There is also an Airbus which runs from Kowloon. Another option is to take the ferry from Pier 7 Hong Kong to Lantau Island.

The new HK Chek Lap Kok is one of the most complete airports I have experienced. It rivals my other two favorite airports which are Schipol in Amsterdam and Changi Airport Singapore.

The Hong Kong Airport consists of two terminals, Terminal One for departures on the upper level and Terminal Two for arrivals. There is a free automatic people mover for transport between terminals.

On my last trip to Hong Kong the airfare was 799.00 USD. But those days are over. Today the cheapest airfare I could find was ASAP.tickets Cathay Pacific 1085.00 USD RT and Korean Air 1159.00 USD RT. There are many airlines offering non-stop flights from the major US cities. Delta Airlines, Continental, United, Singapore, and Thai Air all fly to Hong Kong. ASAP.tickets can be reached at 866-389-8459.

The Hong Kong Airport (HG) opened in 1998. A year earlier, in July 1997, the British officially gave Hong Kong back to the Chinese. Hong Kong remains a capitalist country and little has changed. Hong Kong remains a financial and trade center with growing prosperity. The Hong Kong dollar is the official currency with the exchange rate at 7.80 HKD to 1 USD. It is better to exchange money by using the ATM rather than at the hotel or airport exchange windows. Hong Kong's official language is Cantonese Chinese and English.

There is no lack of hotel rooms in Hong Kong. They pride themselves on well-run hotels and hostels. The

Kowloon side of Hong Kong offers the best prices for the average traveler. I recommend the Hotel Nikko Hong Kong at 72 Mody Rd., Kowloon, HK. 1-866-539-0036. The average nightly rate is 170.00 USD. The room has a city view and premium bedding. There is an LCD television. There is a surcharge for wireless. The hotel has an outdoor pool.

The Hotel Nikko is located in the popular Tsim Sha Tsui district. This area is famous for its shopping in the Harbour City Complex. The Golden mile of Nathan Road is nearby. The Hong Kong Museum of History is within walking distance.

Next on my hotel list is the Kowloon Hotel, 19-21 Nathan Road, Tsim Sha Tsui, Kowloon, HK. The average room rate here is 153.00 USD. Some rooms have a harbour view. There is a surcharge for wireless. The room includes LCD TVs and a minibar. Children eleven years old and younger stay free. The Nathan Road shopping district is a short walk away.

I was on a group tour to China and Hong Kong with SmarTours NYC. Our hotel was the Regal Kowloon Hotel. Great location and view of the harbor in bustling Kowloon. We had a group rate at the Regal.

If you are traveling independently on a limited budget, you may prefer to book sleeping space in a Hostel instead of the more expensive hotel. Hostels are readily available.

A good choice for a hostel is the Hong Kong Hostel, 3F, Block A, 47 Paterson Street, Causeway Bay, Hong Kong. It is located near the bay MTR station. Great location and clean. The rooms are basic but a place to sleep at night. There is A/C and hot water. A good way to save money. Rooms average 25.00 USD. A supermarket is nearby.

Another choice is the Budget Hostel, B5,2F, Block B, 2-4 Kingston Street, Causeway Bay, HK. This hostel offers bunk beds primarily. There is a common area for relaxation and to share stories with fellow travelers. The MTR is right around the corner. The supermarket is across the street. There is A/C and hot water in a shared bathroom. The main entrance is near the corner of Paterson and Kingston Streets. The price in July is 25.57 USD.

The oldest and most famous hostel in Hong Kong is the Chungking Mansions, located at 36-44 Nathan Road in Tsim Sha Tsui, Kowloon, HK. This hostel is well known through the years with backpackers as the cheapest place to sleep in Hong Kong. The building was constructed in 1961. Exit the MTR at exit G.

The Chungking Mansions is composed of many hostels which share different floors in the building. For example, the New International Guest House, Welcome Guest House, and Tokyo/Australian Guest House. The prices can range from 7.50 USD to 15.00 USD. Some rooms appeal to backpackers, while some rooms are occupied by immigrants from the poorer regions of China who are seeking work.

To enjoy some history, stop into the "Red Lips Bar," Tsim Sha Tsui Kowloon, 1A Lock Rd. Many local people call it "the oldest bar in Kowloon." It was made popular by American military men who visited after the Korean War to give "retired ladies of the evening jobs as hostesses.' During the Vietnam War it continued to attract soldiers on RR. Actually, some of the women who work there appear to date from the Vietnam era. But a fun place to visit. A step back in history.

British pubs are popular in Hong Kong because of the British Colonial occupancy. My favorite is Bulldog's Bar and Grill, 66 Mody Road, Kowloon. Tel 2311 6993. It is known for their pub grub such as burgers, meat pies, fish and chips, and the English breakfast. They serve Guinness on tap. The local beers are San Miguel and Tsing Tao. Beer usually costs 50HKD for a pint. The bull dog is a popular gathering place for ex-pats to drink and watch rugby or football.

PJ Murphys is another popular expat pub. Located on 32 Nathan Road, Kowloon, Tel 852 278 23383. PJs portrays itself as an Irish bar. The menu is basic offering: burgers, grilled chicken, and a Sunday Roast Carvery. The Guinness is good and football is on the TV.

For an upscale bar, try out the Dragon1 at the Centrium 60 Wyndam Street, Hong Kong. This is the new hot spot to see and be seen. You may even spot a celeb. There is a bar and dance floor. It also has a dining area named the Red Room, serving Chinese-Japanese fusion dishes. The drinks are pricey.

No visit to Hong Kong is Complete without a lunch or dinner at Jumbo Kingdom floating restaurant in Aberdeen Harbour. The Jumbo has been in Hong Kong for 30 years and has been refurbished recently. It is a popular restaurant with both locals and tourists. Tel 852 2873 7142. Email catherinelam@jumbokingdom.com.

To get to the floating restaurant you go to the Shum Wan Pier, Wong Chuk, HK. There you take a water shuttle.

The food is good but somewhat pricey. The fish and duck are good selections. You select your fish from a tank out back. They offer the usual dim sum if you are just looking for a light lunch. If nothing else, you will be impressed by the ornate décor and overall environment. At night, the restaurant from the outside looks impressive with the decoration of lights.

The Flying Pan is the place to go if you are looking for a 24-hourbreakfast restaurant. Located at 3/F, 81-85 Lockhart Rd, Wan Chai, 2528-9997. They serve breakfast all day plus bloody marys.

Yet another popular pub is Ned Kelly's Last Stand, G/F, 11A Ashley Rd., Kowloon HK. Tel 852-23760562. It is named for one of the most notorious criminals in Australian history. The food is typical pub food such as their famous bushranger hamburger. Most people go to Ned Kelly's for the jazz music which is free each night starting at 9:30 pm. Also, there is a happy hour which runs until 9pm each night. People like the Aussie atmosphere and the drinks. Go early because the pub fills up quickly before the jazz starts.

Another restaurant icon in HK is Jimmy's Kitchen. This restaurant dates from 1928 and many customers call it an old favorite. Jimmy's in HK was opened by Aaron Landau. The original Jimmy's was in Shanghai and was opened by an American serviceman. Today there are two locations in Hong Kong.

G/F South China Bldg.	G/F Kowloon Center
1-3 Wyndham Street	29 Ashley Rd.
Central HK	Kowloon
Tel 2526 5293	Tel 2376

The menu offers a variety of selections ranging from steaks to Chinese fried rice and Indian curries. British grub such as bangers and mash are served as well. They have one of the largest wine lists in Hong Kong. There is a bar with TVs to watch football.

When touring Hong Kong an essential experience is the Star Ferry and the Victoria Peak. Start by boarding the Star Ferry on the Kowloon side. You will see a tourist office where you can pick up a free map. Just walk down Nathan Street and over to Salisbury Road.

Fares for the Star Ferry on either 2.20 HK first class or 1.70 HK second class are very reasonable. Views of the harbour and skyline are incredible and exciting. At night the view is even more exciting.

The movie Suzy Wong (1960) made the Star Ferry and HK harbour popular with people who have never traveled to Hong Kong. Today the Star Ferry is considered a cultural heritage and a public treasure. A must see during a lifetime of travel.

The best way to reach Victoria Peak is by using the tram, the oldest mode of public transportation in HK Island. When you depart the Star Ferry on HK Island, you take a twenty minute walk to the tram station on Garden Road at the base of the peak. The trip to the top of the peak is an exciting experience in itself. The view of the city skyline unfolds beneath you.

The view from the top of Victoria Peak is fantastic! While at the top you may decide to walk around the peak on Lugard Road. The RT Tram ticket is 18 HK. Or you can take the bus down from the peak.

It is a good idea, since you are visiting Victoria Hong Kong Island, to take time to visit and shop in Stanley Market on the south side of the island. Along the way you may decide to stop at the beach at Repulse Bay. Take No. 6 and 6A bus from Central in Hong Kong. There is also a small beach at Stanley if you are packing your bathing suit. Stanley is the area where the Japanese invaded Hong Kong Island in WWII.

Stanley is a small village composed mostly of the English. It is completely different from the best of Hong

Kong and Kowloon. It is a small Chinese town with a western atmosphere.

There are a myriad of shops or stalls in the Stanley market. There are fresh water pearls, luggage, clothing, and trinkets. Be sure to bargain but the shop owners under the tents are hard to bargain with. But it is a nice day outing.

I shall never forget being caught in a heavy rain instantly and taking refuge under a tent. There I met students from HK Baptist University on a field trip. They drilled me with questions about the USA.

Back in Kowloon for shopping, try the night market at Temple Street. Just walk north on Nathan Street. Also there are food vendors. This market is a must see for tourists. While you are on Temple, you might want to shop at the Jade Market. There is no better souvenir or gift from China than Jade. It means "good luck."

A popular tourist excursion is to take the short ferry ride to Lan Tau Island to view the "Big Buddha." This is the largest outdoor Buddha in the world. It is part of the PoLin Monastery. The Buddha is an awe inspiring sight. You reach it by cable car.

Another popular excursion is to visit Guangzhou on mainland China. It is a two-hour train ride. Your hotel travel desk can arrange this trip with joining a small group.

Macau, a former Portuguese colony, is just an hour away from HK by turbojet boat. Macau is a popular gambling haven.

A travel Visa is not needed to visit Hong Kong if you are not staying more than 90 days. A Visa from China is needed to visit mainland China.

Be sure to have an umbrella or hat if you are traveling to HK in July which was my experience. The sun is beating down on you and it rains frequently.

Why visit Hong Kong?

Hong Kong is one of the most dynamic cities in the world. There are numerous restaurants, shops, bars, and sight-seeing to keep you busy for five days or more. It seems HK never sleeps. There is something for everyone.

I leave you with three important Chinese words for use in Hong Kong. Remember protocol is important with the Chinese

Ninhao	Hello
Huanying	Welcome
Xiexie	Thank you

Enjoy! Hong Kong is an exciting destination.

My group tour of China and Hong Kong was with SmarTours. 501 Fifth Ave, Ste 1402, New York, NY 10017. Tel 1-800-337-7773. www.smartours.com. This trip included the Yangtze River Cruise.

32

Final Words: Why I travel

"If you do not have a story to tell then you
have never traveled."
—John Cross

Travel can become an obsession. You can see this from
my many trips. I have visited more than seventy
different countries on all seven continents in my lifetime.
I still get excited about each new trip. Sometimes I think
planning and preparing for a new trip is half the fun. I am
constantly checking airline fares on my computer—always
getting the best deal.

I was first motivated to travel while studying history.
I looked at the photos of the Pyramids or the Taj Mahal
and pledged, "One day I will travel there!" My study of
geography and anthropology further reinforced my desire
to travel. I enjoy experiencing new cultures and the pure
adventure of discovery. Mingling with the people is also
fascinating.

My days of travel almost ended when I was in Patagonia
during the Chilean winter. While hiking in the snow and
ice, I slipped and broke my ankle. It took two years of
operations and rehab to recover enough to travel again.

I will no longer be climbing mountains, but I do love traveling and will continue my quest. Travel is my passion.

Thank you for reading these—my travel stories. I hope they motivate you to go out and build your own memories. May this book inspire you to travel and explore the world. *Vaya con Dios, mi amigo.*

Just go!

Appendix 1

Travel Check List

"When preparing to travel, lay out all your
clothes and all your money. Then take half the
clothes and twice the money."
—Susan Heller

Passport. Is your passport up to date? Most countries have a six-month rule. If your passport expires within six months of your date of arrival, you will be denied entry. Check the expiration date. Make a copy of your passport in case it is lost or stolen.

Travel visa. Some countries require an entry visa. Make sure you meet the entry requirements. Often a country will allow you to purchase the entry visa at the airport upon your arrival at your destination. Best to know before you go though, so find out before you leave.

Travel insurance. You need to protect yourself and your trip costs in case of trip interruption or medical emergency. There are many travel insurance companies. Travel Guard and World Nomads are popular travel insurance options. Use InsureMyTrip.com to compare companies and rates.

Airlines. Shop at least one month or two in advance to secure the best fare. Use Internet travel companies such as Kayak, IATA, Vayama, Travelocity, or Mobissimo. You may prefer to check with a travel agent, but compare the rates before buying. Consolidators are also an alternative. Fly on a Wednesday or Saturday for the best fares.

Travel Health Clinics. Many hospitals offer travel clinics where you can receive vacation or travel medicine. You can Google the Centers for Disease Control and Prevention (CDC) to see if there is a health hazard in the country you plan to visit. You may need malaria pills or a tetanus shot. You can put together your own mini medical kit for travel sickness or diarrhea. Visit your travel clinic six weeks before your departure.

Packing. Weather and the time of the year will determine what you wear on your trip. You'll also need to plan for the activities you plan to do when you're there. You can use WeatherChannel.com to see the weather forecast for your destination. The rule when packing is to pack half of what you will need. Travel light and carry the bare essentials. Make sure you pack toilet paper, a facial washcloth, a rubber sink stopper, sunscreen, a hat, a rain jacket, and an umbrella.

Travel Safety. The State Department web site has a fact sheet for every country, which details current security concerns, areas to avoid, and health risks. To prevent robbery while traveling, use a money belt or a sewn-in clothes pouch to hide your money. Take a lock to lock your backpack or luggage. Split your money between two places. Be sure to use the hotel safe to store your passport, airline tickets, and extra cash. Always be aware of your surroundings.

APPENDIX 2

Packing List

_____ Check or renew passport

_____ Copy of passport

_____ Airline and train tickets

_____ Entry visas

_____ Birth certificate

_____ Travel insurance

_____ Vaccinations, such as malaria or tetanus

_____ Cameras

_____ Battery chargers

_____ Sunglasses

_____ Sunscreen

_____ Light jacket or sweater

_____ Money belt or neck pouch

_____ Walking shoes

_____ Umbrella

_____ Hat

_____ Long underwear

_____ Swim suit

_____ Prescription medicine

_____ Emergency medical kit

_____ Backpack

_____ Carry-on bag

_____ Toilet paper

_____ Motion sickness pills

_____ Copy of itinerary (leave one copy with friends)

_____ Insect repellent

_____ Travel alarm

_____ Travel book

_____ Phrase book

_____ Calculator

_____ Traveler's checks

_____ Student ID Card (ISIC)

_____ Maps

_____ Sanitary napkins

_____ Pain killers/aspirin

_____ Flashlight (torch)

_____ Snacks

_____ Ziplock plastic bags
_____ Men's toiletries
_____ Women's toiletries
_____ Baby bag
_____ Vaccination
certificate
_____ Valuables go in
carry-on bag

_____ T-shirts
_____ Shorts
_____ Socks
_____ Luggage locks
_____ Laundry detergent
_____ First-aid kit with
antibiotic ointment
_____ Aspirin

GLOSSARY

ABTA   Association of British Travel Agents ABTA is a travel trade association based in the UK for tour operators and travel agents. They ensure that travelers have confidence in their travel plans and vacations. They ensure the public gets a fair deal. You can learn more by reading ABTA.com. A traveler can get travel advice and register a complaint. The slogan for ABTA is "Building confidence in travel."

Ali Jinnah (1876-1948) Founder of Pakistan
                His birthday is a national holiday. His mausoleum, his tomb, is a prominent place in Karachi.

Apps   App is computerese shorthand for a software application program. Apps can be downloaded to be used when traveling with a mobile device

App Store   iTunes is the easiest way to add travel apps to your mobile device. Many are free to download. Also Google is popular.

ASTA
American Society of Travel Agents ASTA represents travel professionals and agents and ensures their professionalism and integrity. The emblem of ASTA means you, the traveler, can have confidence in that agent's business dealings. You can book a trip with an ASTA agent with confidence.

Barbuda
Island in Eastern Caribbean. Part of the Antigua Island group. English formed a colony in 1666. "Holding Pens" for slaves. Codrington is the major town.

Bazaar
A Middle Eastern market composed of rows of shops or stalls where trading and bargaining take place.

Bird of paradise
A bird species found mostly in the rain forest of Papua New Guinea. The male is noted for its elaborate and colorful plumage. The male has a long tail. The natives use the plumes in their costumes and rituals.

Bogota
The Capital of Colombia, SA. Cradled in the Andes at 8,612 ft. The largest city of Colombia. Founded in 1538 by the Spanish Colonials. Known for its colonial buildings, cobbled stone streets, churches, museums, and universities. The city radiates out from Plaza de Bolivar at the city center.

Brandenburg Gate—

A well-known landmark in Berlin, Germany. It was built in the eighteenth century as a symbol of peace. It marks the entrance to Unter den Linden and formerly marked the separation of West Germany and East Germany. Atop the gate is the Chariot of Victory.

Byzantine

Refers to the Byzantine Empire, with Constantinople as the capital. It began as part of the Roman Empire. The dates of the Byzantine Empire were AD 330 to AD 1453. Today that same city is called Istanbul and is the capital of Turkey Islam is also prominent today; it is the largest religion in Turkey. About 99 percent of the population is Muslim.

Cabbage Beach Located on Paradise Island, Nassau near the Atlantis Resort. Some call it the most beautiful beach they have seen.

Cancun

Modern and glitzy beachside resorts on the Caribbean, MX. Multistory hotels on beautiful white sandy beaches. Party city.

Cartagena

A port city located on the northern Caribbean coast of Colombia. A popular tourist city. Founded 1533 by Spain. The city was once a pirate haven. The "Old Town" is the most popular tourist attraction with its colonial stone walls. Seafood lovers will enjoy the numerous restaurants.

Cathedral of Monreale
Near Palermo. Most important Duomo in Sicily. Blend of styles. Built in 12th century.

CDC
Centers for Disease Control and Prevention. Located in Atlanta, Georgia, US. 1-800-232-4636, or CDC.gov. An agency of the federal government, the CDC is a good source for travelers' information, such as an advisory of vaccinations needed to visit a country.

CDC
The center for Disease Control and Prevention, Atlanta, USA. Good source of travel health advice. 1-800-232-4636.

Consolidators
Refers to airline travel discount agents who specialize in cheap international tickets. Google airline consolidator or see your travel agent.

Cuyo
The wine-production region of Argentina near Mendoza. Home of malbec grapes.

Diamox
A pill to reduce the incidence of altitude or mountain sickness.

Duomo
Cathedral of Palermo Sicily. Reflects blending of Cultures and Architectural styles.

Eagles Nest   Hitler's Alpine retreat perched on a 6,000 foot peak. Located near the town of Berchtesgaden. Built in 1939 as a birthday gift for Hitler on his 50th birthday.

EC   Eastern Caribbean dollars or currency. Used in Antigua as currency. US dollars is often used as well.

IATA   International Air Transport Association This is a global trade association in the airline industry. 240 airlines are members of IATA. It represents the integrity of airlines around the globe. IATA was founded in Havana, Cuba, in 1945 and is respected worldwide.

Inca   The Incan Empire was located in pre-Columbian South America, primarily in Cuzco, Peru. The culture developed in the twelfth century. The Incas built Machu Picchu. In 1529, Pizarro, a Spanish conquistador, conquered the Incas and plundered their riches.

Inuit   The Eskimo people of North America and Canada.

KAYAK   Computer program to shop and compare best air fares on one site. quick&easy. kayak.com.

KAYAK
It is a popular travel search engine. KAYAK allows you to compare hundreds of travel sites at once. Travelers can compare prices and select the best air fares for their budget. By making comparisons for you, it can save you time and money. KAYAK also can search hotel rates and car rentals. Available also is a mobile phone application.

KAYAK.com/Explore
Explore is a new innovative tool which makes your search for airfares on KAYAK easier. A world map is displayed on your computer screen. The user points the arrow to the travel site he or she is researching. It instantly shows the best price available. It is simple to use. I like the interactive and visual features.

Linderhof
One of "the King's Castles" in Bavaria. Located near Oberamergau.

Loo
Word for toilet.
On the Trans-Siberian express there are two toilets at each end of the train car. There are no showers. Most toilets flush directly onto the tracks below.

Marianplatz
A pedestrian only walkway in the center of Old Munich. Home of many cafes and tourist shops. The New Town Hall and the famous Glockenspiel are found here. Also St. Peter's Church, the oldest in Munich.

Mayan	An ancient civilization that was mostly located in the Yucatán in Mexico. It also spread into Central America. At one time, the Mayan population numbered 15 million. The Mayan civilization began in 2600 BC and rose to prominence by AD 250. They are known for their pyramids, such as Tikal, Coba, Tulum, and Chichen Itza. It is speculated that drought led to their demise.
Merida	City of the ancient land of the Maya, Yucatan, MX. Founded in 13th century A.D. Spanish arrived in 1526.
Moai	Carved stone statues of Polynesians on Easter Island. They have overly large heads in proportion to their bodies. They represent the ancestors of the people. The stone statues are set upright, standing on *ahu*, or stone platforms. One statue can weigh up to eighty-six tons. Each statue represents deity.
Mobissimo	This is a travel website and search engine. The search engine quickly finds and compares cheap airline tickets. The traveler selects the best airfare. This saves time and search efforts. It is very comprehensive and works well for searching international fares.

Namaste   This is a popular greeting used in Nepal
             and India. It is spoken when meeting or
             saying goodbye to another person. The
             hands are pressed together in a prayer-like
             gesture and the greeter bows at the same
             time. It is a cultural gesture. "Namaste"
             literally means "I bow to you."

Nathan Road In the heart of Kowloon. Tsim Sha Tsui
             runs north to south. Important tourist
             attraction with numerous shops and cafes.
             It was the first road built in Kowloon, HK
             in 1861. Once called the Golden Mile.

Nelson's Dockyard - English Harbour. Antigua.
             Part of a National Park which includes
             Shirley Heights. Named for Admiral
             Horatio Nelson who lived there 1784-1787.
             Historical site.

Neuschwanstein
             Most famous castle of "Mad" King
             Ludwig. Bavaria. Built from 1869-1886.
             The ultimate fairy tale castle.

Ottoman   Describing something or someone who is a
             member of the Turkish Ottoman Empire of
             Osmani, who ruled the Ottoman Empire
             from 1603 until World War I.

Pachamama   Goddess, or deity, of the Incas of the
             Andes. Literally means "Mother Earth".
             Cuzco was the center of the Incan Empire.

Potter's Cay   Located beneath the Paradise Island Bridge. Home of numerous food stalls serving up local Bahamian seafood.

Rijksmuseum—A museum located in Amsterdam, the Netherlands. First founded in 1800, it is the Dutch National Art Gallery, containing the Dutch masterpieces of Rembrandt, Vermeer, Frans Hal, and Jan Steen. The museum houses the world famous Rembrandt paining *The Night Watch*. The museum is one of the greatest art museums of the world. It is a must-see. Behind the Rijksmuseum is the Van Gogh Museum.

Star Ferry   This popular ferry carries passengers across Victoria Harbour, HK. It is popular with both locals and tourists. The main route runs between Central HK Island and Tsim Sha Tsui, Kowloon. Inexpensive.

Tannat   A popular wine produced in Uruguay. The tannat grape was introduced by Europeans. This wine has an intense red purple color and has the aroma of cherries. The bodega Bouza is a major producer of tannat wines.

Travel App   Travel aid for use on the mobile device. Examples of Apps are ticketing, hotel rooms, and mapping or GPS. A software application program.

Trojan
: A name which became synonymous with war. The ancient city of Troy and the Trojan warriors were depicted by Homer in *The Iliad*. They showed determination in the defense of the city.

Trojan horse
: The large, fake, hollow horse filled with Greek soldiers who used deception to invade ancient Troy. Today there is a replica outside the city gate.

Trojan War
: A ten-year war between the Greeks and Trojans. The abduction of Helen of Troy by Paris caused the war. It ended with the destruction of Troy. Many tourists visit the ruins of the city.

Tsim Sha Tsui
: Located on the southern tip of Kowloon, HK. Adjacent to Star Ferry and at the bottom of Nathan Road. It is the tourist center of Hong Kong.

Uxmal
: Grand Pyramid of the magician near Merida, MX. Dates from 7th century A.D. Best example of Maya architecture.

Victoria Peak
: A must see on Hong Kong Island. The peak is the highest point in HK. It offers fantastic views over the central point in HK and the harbor. The peak is reached by a tram.

Wan Chai   The Star Ferry operates from the Wan Chai pier on Hong Kong Island. Historically it was the home of "girlie" bars and nightclubs on Jaffe Road, as depicted in the movie "The World of Suzie Wong." Today, after reclamation, it is the home of skyscrapers, public parks, and trade fairs.

BIBLIOGRAPHY

Andrew Bain. *Great Journeys*. Melbourne. Lonely Planet, 2011.

Antigua. Polly Thomas. Thomas Cook Pocket Guides. London. 2009. Thomas Cook Publishing.

Baird, David. Frommer's 2010 Cancun, Cozumel and the Yucatan. New York: Wiley, 2009.

Baird, Frommer's Cancun and the Yucatan. 2012. Wiley Publishers. Hoboken, N.J.

Beezley, The Oxford History of Mexico. 2010. Oxford University press UK. Oxford.

Bellows, Keith. Editor. *Journey of a Lifetime: 500 of the Worlds Greatest Trips*. Washington, D.C. National Geographic, 2007.

Brainy Quote. Book Rags Media Network. Copyright @ 2001-2013 BrainyQuote.com.

Brash, Celeste. The Travel Book: A Journey Through Every Country in the World, 2nd ed. Melbourne. Lonely Planet, 2011.

Burkholder, Mark A., and Lyman L. Johnson. Colonial Latin America, 2nd ed. New York: Oxford University Press, 1994.

CNNTV Travel. 50 Ultimate travel apps NYC. June 2013.

Fein, Juide. Life is a *Trip: The Transformative Magic of Travel*. Santa Fe, New Mexico: Garcia Street Books, 2010.

Franz, The Peoples Guide to Mexico. John Muir Publications. Santa Fe, New Mexico. Revised 1988

Frommer's. Pauline Frommer's *Spend Less See More Travel Tips*. New York: Frommer's 2012.

Galicka, Munich and the Bavarian Alps. DK Travel Guides. 2004. London

GHS-Inc. "Top Five Secrets to Savy Travel." Conde Nast Traveler. New York. URL. 2011.

How to chew Betel Nut in Papua New Guinea. Wikihow. Last modified June 15, 2011. http://www.wikihow. com/Chew-Betel-Nut-in-Papua-New-Guinea.

Humphreys, Rob. *The Pocket Rough Guide Prague*. Berkeley: Rough Guides, 2011.

Kepnes, How to Travel the World on $50 a day: Travel Cheaper, Longer, Smarter. Penguin Group. USA. N.Y. 2013

Korfmann, Manfred O. *Troia/Wilusa Guidebook: A Site on the UNESCO World Heritage List*. Canakkale Turkey. Tubingen, 2005.

Lipscomb, Adrian, John Murray, and Rowan McKinnon. *Papua New Guinea (Lonely Planet Travel Guides)*. Melbourne. Lonely Planet, 1998.

Lonely Planet. *1000 Ultimate Experiences,* London: Lonely Planet, 2009.

Machlin, Milt. *The Search for Michael Rockefeller*. Pleasantville, NY. Common Reader/Akadine Press, 2001.

O'Reilly, James, editor. *The Best Travel Writing 2010: True Stories from Around the World*. Palo Alto, CA.Solas Press, 2010.

PCmagazine.com. 10 sites for cheap flights. 2013.

Quotes about Travel. Good Reads.com. URL. 2012.

Raub, Lonely Planet Columbia 6ed. 2012. Melbourne, Australia.

Reader, John. Kilimanjaro. London: Elm Tree Books, 1982.

Rick Steves' Istanbul, Aran and Aran. New York. Avalon Travel Publishing, 2008.

Santella, Chris. *Once in a Lifetime Trips: The Worlds 50 most Extraordinary and Memeorable Travel Experiences.* New York: Clarkson Potter/Random House, 2009.

Schulte, Peevers, Munich, Bavaria and the Black Forest. Lonely Planet 3ed. 2008. Hawthorn Australia

Stellin, Susan. *How to Travel Practically Anywhere.* Boston: Houghton Mifflin, 2006.

Steves, Rick. *Rick Steves' Best of Europe 2012.* New York: Avalon Travel Publishing, 2012.

Steves, Munich, Bavaria and Salzburg. 2011. Avalon Travel. Berkeley, CA. USA

Steves, Rick. *Rick Steves' Pocket Athens.* New York: Avalon Travel Publishing, 2012.

Taylor, Kerry. "Travel Check List." Squawkfox. 2012.

"The 50 most inspiring travel quotes of all time." Matador Network. Last modified December 19, 2011. http://matadornetwork.com/bnt/50-most-inspiring-travelquotes-of-all-time/.

Thomas, The Conquest of Mexico. 1993. Pimlico Random House. London UK.

"Top Five Secrets to Savvy Travel." Condé Nast Traveler. 2012.

Vecchio, Frommer's Sicily 5ed. Wiley. 2011. West Sussex, UK.

Wilkinson. Let's Go Southeast Asia. 1999. St. Martin's Press New York

Zaraysky, Susan. Travel Happy, Budget Low. Cupertino, CA. Kaleidomundi, 2009.

INDEX

C

Z